THE EIGHT LEGGED ATOMIC DUSTBIN WILL EAT ITSELF

THE EIGHT LEGGED ATOMIC DUSTBIN WILL EAT ITSELF

by
Martin Roach

Independent Music Press

LONDON

First published in the U.K. in 1990 by
Uncle John Press
This impression 1992
Order No. UJ1024

Every effort has been made to credit the photographers' material in
this book, however a few were unobtainable. The publishers would be
grateful if any ommissions were brought to their attention.

ACKNOWLEDGMENTS:

The author would like to express extreme gratitude to the following people who have all contributed to this book, despite having far more important things to do:

Jonn, Mat, Clint, Alex, Rat, Dan, Tank, Miles, Martin, Martin, Malcolm, Paul

Craig, Rod and Richard at Chapter 22

Paul Aston, Paul Bolton, Bones, Neil Booth, Phil Creed, Dave Crook, Chris Fradgeley, Steve Fellows, Kevin Gammond, Jane Houghton, Les Johnson, Sam Jukes, Dave Morris, Laura Nicol, Robin Okey, Harold Parsons, Mark Smith, Dave Travis, Paul Quinn.

Pop Will Eat Itself Photos by Dave Travis.
Ned's Atomic Dustbin Photos by Neil Booth.

Design by Terrapin Design

Stuart, Joe, Trudi, Harco and Stu Coles

Special thanks to Mom and Dad.

CONTENTS

INTRODUCTION

I'm from Stourbridge. It's no big deal. Everyone's got to come from somewhere, Sir.

Pop Will Eat Itself, The Wonder Stuff and Ned's Atomic Dustbin are said to come from Stourbridge and in a way they do, because people say they do. But in reality it's one of those romantic myths that makes life more interesting than it really is.

All three bands contain members that come from Stourbridge or it's local surroundings. However, they also contain members who are not, who never were, who no longer live in, who do not wish to be associated with or in one case has never been to Stourbridge!

What the point is, however, is that Stourbridge was an early base for all three bands and their respective members. Most of us lived, rehearsed, played our first gigs and drank here. Probably the contact addresses on our first demo tapes were 'Stourbridge'. That in itself, considering the success and influence that the three bands enjoy, is interesting, at least to anyone who likes one or more of the bands.

This book isn't about a 'scene', because there is no such cliche. It isn't trying to create or perpetuate a modern day myth. It's just the chronicle of an oddity. An oddity that three bands should break out of a modest Black Country town and come to mean a fair amount to a fair amount of people.

Basically, if you're interested read on. If you're not, put this book down and we'll stop wasting each others time.

Clint

PWEI STOURBRIDGE 1991

DRAMATIS PERSONAE

FROM EDEN:

	CLINT	Vocals, Guitar
	ADAM	Guitar, Keyboards
	CHRIS	Bass
	MALCOLM	Guitar, Vocals
	MILES	Drums
then	GRAHAM	Drums

POP WILL EAT ITSELF:

	CLINT	Vocals, Guitar
	ADAM	Guitar, Keyboards
	RICHARD	Bass
	GRAHAM	Vocals
then	FUZZ	Drums

THE WONDER STUFF:

	MILES	Vocals, Guitar
	MALCOLM	Guitar, Vocals
	MARTIN	Drums
	BOB	Bass
	MARTIN	Fiddle, Banjo, Accordion
then	PAUL	Bass

NED'S ATOMIC DUSTBIN:

	JONN	Vocals
	MAT	Bass
	ALEX	Bass
	RAT	Guitar
	DAN	Drums

POP WILL EAT ITSELF

"It's really all about jumping up and down. We're just having a good time and we want everyone jumping. All the good punk bands are really about jumping. Even with the Clash... they were jumping up and down." CLINT

CHAPTER ONE

· "We were at college - a group of 15 and 16 year olds into the Banshees and The Stranglers, The Psychedelic Furs, into punk and bands generally." Spending most of their college hours pursuing girls rather than academic excellence, Clint Mansell and Co. were always far more interested in bands: "...the sort of kids who queued up for hours, then ran to the prime spot in front of the stage, and refused to move from that exact spot. We didn't realise that if you were tough you stuck at the bar all night, and then, as The Clash came on, you barged down the front and told someone 'hey mate, your mom's on the 'phone..'"[1] It was at one of their many excursions to gigs that the first mention of starting a band was made - "A group of us went to see the Banshees in Malvern, and Chris Fradgeley and Malcolm Treece were trying to get a band together so they asked me and Adam if we were interested, even though we'd never done anything before." Up to that point, Clint had nurtured only one other ambition on the stage: "I can remember, before the Poppies, having the idea of getting up on stage by myself and just twanging rubber bands. I didn't in the end because I realised that while it may be quite a radical idea it would accomplish very little."[2]

"So we started rehearsing and it was terrible to begin with - I was so scared of singing I went in the next room and sang on my own with this massive lead all over the place. Really bad. We were short of a drummer, I couldn't sing at all and it was going nowhere. Malc and Chris had some nice tunes but nothing we could really sort out. So we advertised for a drummer and Miles Hunt answered it - he must have been about $2^{1}/2$ at the time I think, I mean I was only 18. He was a great drummer, but we didn't really rehearse enough. In the meantime they had tried two other singers behind my back because I was so bad. Chris told me about this and asked me to try these three new songs, which was pretty sound of him really, as things turned out. " This was with hindsight, a wise choice, but not one that Clint's frustrated academic superiors would approve of: "Clint, as the world knows, only joined a band in the first place so he could go back and tell all his old school teachers that they were wrong all those years ago when they told him he'd never make anything of himself. And he has of course, but will they be impressed with 'head grebo of a spotty pop group' as credentials."[3]

Originally called 'Flowers From Eden' the newly abbreviated 'From Eden' rehearsed for nine months, gigged a handful of clubs and then split to produce two of the most successful bands of the decade: Pop Will Eat Itself and The Wonder Stuff. At this early stage however, Clint remembers there was little or no indication of the potential of those involved. "We hadn't got a clue, although the music was quite good for the time, sort of pre-gothic, like The Psychedelic Furs with a Banshees guitar." Their first gig was at The Broadway in Stourbridge, on July 13th, 1982, some time after which they supported The Sisters of Mercy in Selly Oak. "At the time the Sisters weren't really well known, but the week after we supported them they were on the front cover of Sounds magazine. I think we were the only ones who'd heard of them, 'cos we'd seen their singer, Andy Eldridge, at a gig in Huddersfield.The only other support of a real band we did was The Membranes in Stafford, and John Robb remembers us to this day. It was 1982 and we used to really dress up for the gigs - we were into Bauhaus and stuff, almost glammy, sort of fun." One local newspaper described them as "hard-look image, with black leather and rough-and-tumble haircuts," whilst a more critical reviewer saw them as "living out the dated macho rockstar/guitar hero fantasy, playing shapeless self-important rock." Nevertheless, over the course of the next year they proceeded to develop a sufficient enough following and good press to suggest that they were "one of the finest bands in the area and would surely earn accolades galore wherever they grace the boards..wake up to what you're missing."[4]

Good reviews aside however, it was clear that the band wasn't really working - there was little new material being written and it

wasn't gelling effectively. It was at this stage that Miles left to form another band called The Wonder Stuff. "He was going to leave anyway but we were all mates so we were a bit upset really. The last gig we did with Miles was in Nottingham - it was good stuff but what really let it down was my voice. I was trying to do too much, more than I do now in fact, but that's all part of finding out what you can and can't do. After the split for a while Miles was going to have all his hair cut off, get a proper job and never play music again. Anyway, we started writing new stuff for 'From Eden' and advertised for a drummer - the first person to reply after three months was Graham ("a grubby, evil minded Phil Collins for today's hip hop highway."[5]). He had his first rehearsal and then gave up his job the same night - he was well into it. There was only Malc who had a job, working for West Midlands Coinmatics emptying fruit machines." Even with this new line-up however it was still not right. There was a brief flirtation with a manager - "aright berk" - and disillusionment began to set in as the band polarised musically.

"We started to get rockier and rockier - it got so ridiculous that Chris was into Bryan Adams at one point! So one night we arranged a meeting at The Mitre pub - before we went, King and The Three Johns were on The Tube. Me and Graham thought that King was terrible but the Three Johns were great; we go down the pub and Malc and Chris thought King was great and hated The Three Johns -that said it all really so we split up. There was no animosity - it just wasn't working. You have got to get the right personalities in there - even if you disagree, if you respect someone's opinion then you have to give them a bit of leeway. If they're into Bon Jovi and you're into UK Subs then you may have a problem, but if you're into similar stuff then you need to give and take. Me and Gra don't always see eye to eye, but you have to let an idea go and see how or if it works. You can't just say 'no way'. That's all about compromises between the four of us really." Brum Beat Magazine recorded the band's passing with some regret: "One of the area's most powerful live acts is no more, although Clint, Adam and Graham are sticking together and seeking to re-explore the original spirit of the band."[6]

This new band 'Wild and Wandering' proved to be a far more

successful venture than the previous one. At this early stage the band were clear where their priorities lay - "We saw The Three Johns on the Tube having fun and we wanted to do that. We really liked Wasted Youth, so we did a load of their covers and some old 'From Eden' numbers to have a laugh. The problem we've always had is that when we say that, people think we're not serious, like the musical version of The Three Stooges - we just really wanted to enjoy what we were doing and okay, being an arsehole on stage sometimes, but basically having a laugh." Ironically, some people viewed the band in the opposite light - "when Poppies say Grrr!!! came out (the band's self-produced debut E.P), they saw us as some kind of thinking man's pop, while all we ever have been is a bunch of long haired guys who like to entertain people and get pissed, preferably both at the same time." Graham quickly laughs off these suggestions - "them days were our chaos days, when we'd make a point of never finishing a gig. Always finished our beers mind." "We're just taking it a stage further from standing in front of the mirror with our tennis racquet's, basically." "After every performance we don't sit analysing it in the dressing room, we head for the bar, or for the promoter for the money for the bar. We're not that serious." At the end of the day "...it's all an excuse to go for a curry , rush out without paying and nick the hubcaps from the ol' bastard down the road."[7] Clint, even now, finds the overly serious attitude of some young bands tiresome: "Each to their own but these bands who stand there looking pretentious are just rubbish, I just think 'Grow up'. That was one of the first things I liked about the Neds, they were really happy-go-lucky and had no pretensions about themselves. In Japan (June 1991), there was this magazine with loads of bands on the cover and Ride were on there with a perfectly posed, airbrushed photo, beautifully lit. Don't get me wrong we've all done those sort of posey photos now and again, but the next-door photo was the Ned's who you could see were basically thinking to themselves 'bollocks' - it was great. I hate that sort of posey thing."

Despite their easy-going attitude the band gradually began to attract some attention. "We'd done some gigs in London as Wild and Wandering by this time and met some Southern business-

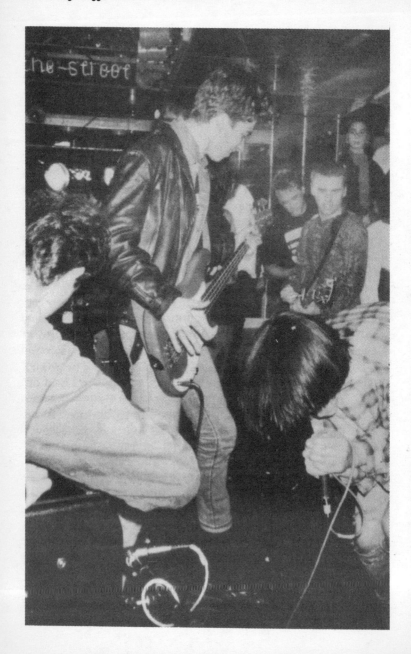

types and thought that they were real dickheads. We needed a bass player, so we advertised and after we'd met a couple of people who weren't really happening, we mentioned it to Rich, a good friend from Stourbridge, who completed the line-up. He was a pretty good musician so that really helped us along. Basically at this stage we were absolutely legless at every gig. There were a lot of quite serious bands around at the time, so when we came on and were drunk *and* crap, at least it was different." It was at this time that the band got hold of a Portastudio from a friend - Clint remembers how they immediately felt at home with the four track and started to add new elements to their music. "We started putting stuff down that was not in the songs live and it was great fun really." They also experienced their first taste of rejection - "We sent out a load of demos and this guy from Reflex Records in Malvern wrote back saying he was really interested, but we never bloody heard from him again. So we decided to do a single of our own called 'Dust Me Down', a very slow one, very 1985 I suppose. As it happened we met these blokes from Rich Bitch Studios in Selly Oak who said they were trying to set up a label and would help us out. So we recorded it there, but for some reason it took about eight months to come out. We'd recorded it in the summer of 1985 and had borrowed some money from the Enterprise Allowance Scheme; so I paid off a band loan from my Dad with the £80 per week I was getting on the scheme. As soon as Rich Bitch expressed an interest we weren't really qualified for any allowance and they came down really heavy on us - at one point I was up for fraud. We got out of it somehow."

"The single was due to come out in the January of 1986 - in the meantime we'd seen this advert in Melody Maker for a one-off auction of loads of gear down in London, so we thought we've got to scrape enough together to get this one Portastudio for about £250. Where we got the car to go to London from I don't know - we piled down there early one morning but when we got there we were about fourtieth in the queue. We were so pissed off because we thought we'd missed it. Anyway somehow Gra managed to force his way in and we got it."

"The portastudio was kept over at Gra's moms, and he basically went mental on it. We were listening to The Jesus and Mary Chain, early Primal Scream, The Shop Assistants and stuff like that and suddenly Graham had written loads of songs in about three days . With a few I'd done, that was to form the basis of all the early PWEI stuff, songs like 'UHU', 'Mesmerised', 'Psychopath In My Soup', 'Summergirl', 'Spunk Bubbles', 'Devil Inside', 'Run Around', and some stuff that's never been released. So suddenly we had a set of say fifteen songs, that were nothing like what we had done with Wild and Wandering. Rich Bitch approached us again and wanted us to do an album for FM Revolver, but we wanted to do this five track single in a brown paper bag as a little package. We'd realised that we had some really good stuff, unbelievably substantial and clever. Between the four of us we had the strength to feel we could do it, and all these people who were slagging us off were basically arseholes anyway. Everybody told us 'you can't change your name from Wild and Wandering, you've had a review and everything ' and we said 'why?'. Even now we're told not to do this, and not to do that and we still have to say 'why?'." "We've always said that the important thing is to make the kind of sound that we want to hear...We know that we could make more commercial music, Inspiral Carpets and the Stone Roses are so popular because they are easy on the ear. You haven't got to be that clever to eye up what's in the charts and see what the formula is, but that isn't really why you do it. I mean, when have the charts ever been a yardstick of what's good. It's great to be in the charts but it's no measure of whether a record's any good any more."[8]

So PWEI as it exists today was born - except for the name: "The new demo was ready but we couldn't decide on the name we were going to use. We had three - 'Pop Tarts', 'Grrr!!' and 'Pop Will Eat Itself'. So we sent the demos to all these people and said the first one that comes back to us we'll use that name. John Robb of the Membranes sent us a letter back from his Vinyl Drip Records and said what a great name - so that was that. The name itself was in an interview with a band called Jamie Wednesday in the NME, two of whom are now Carter USM as it happens, and David Quantick was waxing lyrical about the state of pop music and how it regurgitates itself, and how, if you take it to its logical extreme, you'll have the perfect pop song with all the best bits in it, and so pop will eat itself. That really fitted what we were doing because at the time it was all basically nicked. When you look back it all seems so rosy, especially since we're doing okay now, but at the time we were so depressed some nights doing that demo. I remember late one night when we were doing a Hawkwind song called 'Orgone Accumulator' and we'd finished all the drums and stuff, basically the whole song, down at Gra's Mom and Dad's. We went in to another room to do the vocals because we thought they sounded better in there (as you do in a very George Martin sort of way), and Gra wiped the drums off, clean off at about two in the morning. We got it done anyway."

At this point the band got to know fellow Midlanders The Mighty Lemon Drops - they swapped demos and liked each other's stuff, so the Lemon Drops arranged some gigs for them. This coincided with the release of their first E.P, 'Poppies Say Grrr!!!', recorded at Lanes End Studio in Studley. "We went for this five track E.P with name and tracks only on it. It cost us all told about £350, and took 14 hours, at some studio well out in the country. To listen to the record now the sound isn't that great but it did the job at the time. We found a shop in Birmingham that sold brown paper bags and bought 500 for £2-something, along with a John Bull Printing kit, and spent a day stamping it all out - they looked great and we could sell 'em at a pound a piece. Adam was equally enthusiastic : " I think ours (was) the first truly independent record to come to people's attention since..Bill Grundy's EP 'The TV Personalities'."⁹

Clint at the time was sharing a flat with Miles Hunt in Colleygate. As Miles recalls "Clint would be out EVERY night and he seemed to know everybody. Clint had some classic lines like 'Hello JB's, Home of the stars.' All very cynical of course. He was a good frontman...brilliant. PWEI seemed to have a much better time than we ever did. They were changing their style all the time and just larking about. The rest of us were just buggering about trying to get bands going with no real success. It was the Poppies who brought it all off really. Everything that was going right for them was down to their personalities - it was so much fun to go to see them because of the characters involved."

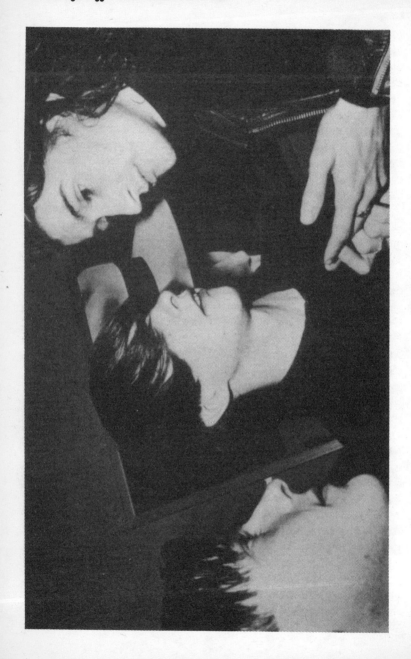

"That night he came home with the Portastudio tape was brilliant. When they made their own record it got them reactions all over the place. All the time there was this really great vibe coming off them that they were always having a brilliant time. Then suddenly, instead of being locally successful, they were doing national stuff and people like Bobby Gillespie (of Primal Scream) were phoning them up. They were really into it; for example, one day they heard John Peel was going to be at a gig at Birmingham Polytechnic, so they went there in the afternoon, found him out and said 'Here's our record.' Peel took it back to London and played it on his show that night. It was brilliant."

Clint continues the story: ""Me and Miles had this flat together and they were starting to get The Wonder Stuff off the ground at the same time. The debut single was released on 16th May, 1986 - we'd had our first gig on the Friday, May 2nd at The Mere in Stourbridge and a couple of nights before The Stuffies had done their first gig at JB's. The night the single came out we were also playing JB's - we went down well and sold a few copies."

One Birmingham promoter, Dave Travis, remembers many early PWEI gigs in the lesser venues of the second city: "The gig at Mega's Wine Bar that lasted six minutes because Clint had had enough was a classic - they had to play in the corridor down the side of the toilets, so if anybody needed the loo they had to walk right in front of the band. Not many did mind you, 'cos there were only 15 people there." Rich remembers an equally dreadful gig: "One night we were playing somewhere and I suddenly realised I couldn't hear Adam. I looked into the audience and he was dancing at the front of the stage. We had a bit of a debate about that one..."[10] Travis once arranged to meet the band at a local party to talk about some dates and drink beer - they were two hours late - "We'd arranged to meet in The Trafalgar in Moseley but they waited for me in The Nelson in Sparkhill. I got some idea of the band when I found them choosing clothes from a selection of open dustbins the morning after a particularly rough party. The next time we went out Graham was using the phone in Burberry's when Clint decided to pull him away, taking the phone with him. That cost them another £85. Even at this stage you could have done a cartoon about PWEI, only it would

probably have been X-rated."

Clint remembers their first air play on local radio (BRMB), was soon followed by greater things. "At the time Janice Long had been doing a piece about 'how to make your own record', that sort of thing, so Ad wrote to her and said he'd followed her advice and made a single, here it is. Amazingly she played 'Psychopath in My Soup' on the radio that night, then gave it to John Peel who played it to open his show. I didn't hear either because we'd had a gig. What happened there was we sent a record to a guy called Martin Whitehead in Bristol who ran Subway Records and he phoned us back saying 'this is the best record I've ever heard in my life, come down and have a gig.' It all started to click all at once. Anyway, I got home after this gig and I was chatting away to my girl friend and she said 'by the way Janice Long played your record last night...' I couldn't believe it. Around the same time The Lemon Drops passed a copy on to some journalist who made it single of the week in the NME. John Peel continued to play more tracks, and we continued doing gigs. Rich's phone was suddenly red hot - we did gigs anywhere. We did one in Lincoln for £25, absolutely skint. We supported The Razor Cuts for £20 but we just wanted to play to people and get the experience of these gigs. Terry Staunton was at one of those early gigs to give the band their first NME review: "Right this next song's called 'Everyone's getting a John Peel session except for us so we're going down the pub for our own.' Take it away men." Snap goes the snare drum, crackle goes a very dodgy bass amp, and PWEI go GRRR!!! at a nonplussed Friday night crowd somewhat depleted since the last bus left half an hour ago...What we have here is four lads with a handful of songs of such brevity that they make The Ramones look like The Alan Parsons Project. The Poppies offer a neat line in naivety, a subtle blend of baby-faced innocence and biting wit blazing a trail through 30 minutes of pure fun."[11]

The band eventually got their first Peel session on 17th June 1986, after The Lemon Drops had been forced to pull out of their slot and had put forward PWEI as a replacement. "We went mad 'cos this was the thing we'd always wanted to do. Gra was still churning out the   numbers, so we did 'Sweet Sweet Pie',

'Inside Out','Demolition Girl', and 'Oh Grebo I Think I Love You.' We'd done a gig supporting Yeah God on the night and when I got back Miles got up and had taped it, so we played it at about four in the morning. Peel had gone mad about it, we were well chuffed. At that point we felt unstoppable, like we can do something here." The band had got some press by this stage but the E.P. was still only available on mail order. Then Nine Mile Cartel got in touch, arranged distribution and it went in at No.17 in the Independent charts. "The funny thing was we'd approached The Cartel earlier and they weren't interested at all. We'd been to them as Wild and Wandering with this 7" and they'd said '7" doesn't sell.' We argued that there must be a lot of other people who are as skint as us and would go for a record for a quid rather than a £3 12". But they didn't want to know - fair enough, but I always felt that Indie labels should have room for a bit of enterprise as well as business."

"We'd set up this record label called Desperate because that's what we were. The songs at this point were coming out of our ears. I was nowhere near as prolific as Gra, never have been, but between us we were really churning it out. I had another demo at home of eighteen unreleased tracks, there were only five on the Peel session." It was prior to this that Chapter 22 Records first heard about the band it was going to sign and eventually manage. Clint recalls the unorthodox sales pitch they used to tempt Craig Jennings, Director of Chapter 22: "When we were in Wild and Wandering, Brum Beat Magazine really liked us for our ' irreverent wit and humour', that sort of stuff. Balaam and the Angel, Chapter 22's first band, who are good guys,and ourselves had a bit of girlfriend trouble so there was a bit of rivalry there, even though they were doing really well. Anyway, one afternoon me and Rich were 'round his house and we got absolutely legless on some home-made wine. In Brum Beat Magazine that week there were loads of bits about us and nothing about Balaam and the Angel. So Rich phoned up Chapter 22, absolutely legless and said: 'Ah, yes, I've just been reading Brum Beat and there's loads of things about my band and there's absolutely nothing about your band Balaam and the Angel so how come you haven't signed us yet' and put the phone down on him.

It was Craig and he had an absolute fit."

By now PWEI had developed something of a reputation for their live show: "Next come PWEI, wearing their usual leather jackets and long hair, but minus their trousers. They have socks stuffed down their pants, creating bulges and bumps of impossible proportions. Could this be what they mean by Poppiecock? Probably not, but it's part of what makes the Poppies so exceptionally entertaining; they really couldn't give a stuffed Y-front about what is and is not acceptable behaviour, good or bad taste, ideologically sound or unsound." Another reviewer was already making lofty predictions - "as anyone who has seen their live shows over the past year knows, their sound and their songs have been developing behind people's backs into something with all the hallmarks of great pop-rock." Clint sees it rather more simply: "It's really all about jumping up and down. We're just having a good time and we want everyone jumping. All the good punk bands are really about jumping. Even with the Clash..they were jumping up and down."[12]

It was at one of these gigs that Jennings decided to sign the band. "While we were Wild and Wandering we'd met Dave Travis who used to manage Terry and Jerry and The Man Upstairs, and he liked us. At a party in Brum he swapped us ten singles for ten cans of lager ('Import Premuim'), which for us at the time was a really good deal. He really liked it and, as he was promoting Burberry's Club, he got us a slot with The Shop Assistants who had asked for us to support them. At that time we used to come on to 'Badman' by The Cockney Rejects, 'cos we really liked it, and we happened to play a great gig (The Shop Assistants were impressed enough to give PWEI an extra £30 on top of their already handsome appearance fee of £20). A few people were getting to know our stuff by then - we were still basically playing gigs drunk, but because by now we'd had quite a lot of practice we started to get it together. This is when we started to headbang a bit as well, 'cos at the time everyone else had really short hair. Fortunately, Craig of Chapter 22 was there and loved it, so we had a meeting and he loved the demos we had. It seemed like they could do a good job and they were Midlands so we went for it. Jennings remembers the first time he saw the band

"I saw them at Burberry's and thought I've just got to get involved; it wasn't that I thought they could make shitloads of cash, it was just that I thought they were absolutely brilliant. The Poppies always had that pioneering punk-rock spirit that I liked. They did what they wanted to do and I admired that - from a manager's point of view that's very lucky to be so into what you're doing."

PWEI continued to frequent the local and national gig circuits: in 1986 they played 56 gigs and supported bands such as The Mighty Lemon Drops, Yeah God, The Bodines, The Shop Assistants, The Wedding Present and Balaam and The Angel. PWEI's penchant for live shows began to materialise at this stage - any new material was backed up by prolific gigging. "We played at least three or four gigs every week, mostly arranged by ourselves. One night we supported The Lemon Drops in Newcastle and the next night the Bodines in Brighton; that's a bloody long way I can tell you, but we had nothing else to do, we got enough to cover the petrol and we loved it. We used to sleep in the back of the van and get our hands on anything alcoholic we could and sleep that off in the back of the bus. That's how we got the thing about us all being smelly 'cos we'd be on these two mattresses in this van, and you didn't really wash a great deal unless you happened to pass a Little Chef or something. It wasn't exactly hygienic but it got us known - the gigs that is, not being smelly. We played to loads of people like this." Graham puts it more poetically: "The nicotine used to condense on the van ceiling and then drip into your face when you were asleep."[13]

"We'd released the single in May and come the summer we were gigging like mad. Chapter 22 wanted a new single in October so we had planned to do a 7" five track with 'The Black Country Chainstore Massacre', 'Oh Grebo..' and three others. On the 12" we put the first single on the B-side to make 10 tracks." This was recorded at The Barn Studios in Leamington Spa and released on 27th October as 'Poppiecock'. "It was a great deal really and people seemed to love it. On the night of the release , we were third on the bill to The Shop Assistants and My Bloody Valentine. We came off stage and heard the single had gone straight in the Indie charts at No.5 - we couldn't believe it,

and then we had to go and sleep in the van outside. We were getting on great with Craig, he was into all the same stuff as us and he then said he wanted to manage the band. We thought great because he was virtually doing that anyway, and to this day we've never signed anything with him, it works out great. He got us with ITB agency first and then some more interviews. The third single was recorded in November - it was essentially live, we could probably have done an album in three days."

'Sweet Sweet Pie' was released in January 1987 and there was a twenty eight day tour arranged to promote the single, during which the band had their own soundman for the first time. Clint says this all helped to polish their act, but he sympathised with the newcomer - "Sal didn't know what was going on. The first night Ad beat the shit out of me because I'd been an arsehole for some time, and fully deserved it, so I was covered in cuts and bruises for the first three or four gigs. Craig was drunk, me and Ad were fighting and he was sitting there facing another month of this. Anyway it worked out." The audience, however, refused to be outdone by the band - after only a handful of gigs there was a major crowd fight causing the police to be called in, as a result of which PWEI were fined.

With such Independent chart success it was perhaps only a matter of time before PWEI were going to attract major label interest. CBS came, they saw but they didn't sign. "We'd just had the 'Sweet Sweet Pie' video on the Whistle Test, watched it in the bar, on national T.V, thought we'd made it, then gone on stage at Cardiff in front of about 70 people - a sort of 'don't get cocky mate.' When CBS came to see us we were wearing great coats and I did the whole gig with my back to the audience - this A&R bloke was not impressed at all. To a certain extent it was a blessing in disguise because although we were pig sick about it at the time, if they'd signed us then we wouldn't have known what we were doing and they probably wouldn't have let us develop like we have. We just weren't ready - I'd have put money on us lasting no more than six months."

The E.P's were then released across Europe, followed by a small tour of Switzerland, Holland, Germany and France, which has now acquired almost legendary notoriety for PWEI's off-stage contributions as much as for the shows themselves. Europe's first taste of PWEI nights out saw Adam taking an unnatural liking for a shoe polishing machine, a mass destruction of a varied array of rubber plants and two Poppies dancing stark naked in a Dutch nightclub. Camper Van Beethoven suffered the unenviable fate of having PWEI riding bicycles across the stage during their set and hotels found it all too much to handle. In one instance what finally did it was Kerry the roadie testing out various contraceptives for size on the hotel landing whilst each bed appeared to have far too many occupants. This was probably the first time that the press latched onto the band as perfect pop gossip column contributors. It all helped to create media attention; take for example this exert from Record Mirror: "What the Poppies manage to do, of course, is to resurrect the irresponsible rock and roll lifestyle that has fallen out of fashion in the past few years. These mouthy Black Country boys slot effortlessly into that tradition which honours The Stones widdling against a garage wall; Led Zeppelin's hotel thrashing exploits and Jim Morrison's onstage willie-waving shows...PWEI are perfecting the art of waywardness with considerable zest." Alternatively, as a grateful Adam suggests "I wouldn't even know what I've done in the last week otherwise..."[14]

Clint remembers the distinct lack of money despite the band's relative success. "Sounds magazine came out with us and we got our first front cover in Holland, but we were still on the dole and the records weren't making any money. It wasn't until we got back from Europe and Craig had got us a publishing deal with RCA, that we could afford to sign off our £25 a week and get £80 - it seemed like loads of cash. We were gigging, getting paid, making records and thinking 'this is the business.'" Clint was clearly never going to lose touch of reality: "If someone wants to give us £25 to drive up the motorway to play fifteen minutes of crappy pop music that's fine. If they want to pay us 300 quid, give us crates of beer and send us to Germany to do it...even better." Even if that early European tour was not exactly lucrative it proved to be a crucial influence on the Poppies musically. "While we were in Europe we went to a lot of clubs and really started to get into the whole dance thing, even Madonna. By now we were a

little bored with our old stuff 'cos we'd gigged these songs for so long. We felt that the previous format was limiting and that some of the new stuff was sounding like retreads of older numbers."

On returning from Europe they recorded an ill-fated new demo - "That session just didn't have it, the studio just wasn't right for the sound we were looking for, so we had to have a re-think. We had two goes at the new single and it just didn't work - in the end we recorded 'Picnic in the Sky', 'There Is No Love Between Us Anymore','Inside You' and a cover of a Shriekback song called 'Everything That Rises'. By this time, we were playing 'F1-11' live. We'd just heard 'Raising Hell', the Run DMC album and absolutely loved it. Gra said we should try 'F1-11' along the same lines, instead of the thrashy way it was at the time. We tried it and it seemed to work. Craig agreed it was worthy of a single, so we went to a studio where we knew they could pro-grame drums - Stanway Studios in Wednesbury - it worked a treat and it was done in a day. We also did 'Everything That Rises' again, and 'Orgone Accumulator' ("We liked bits of the song but we couldn't be bothered playing eleven minutes so we just took the best bits out.") and 'Like an Angel'- we put that out as a four track single of covers. It got to No.75 in the charts and No.1 in the Indies and The Chart Show put the video on, it was great. Chapter 22 financed everything and it worked a treat." This release was only a prelude to the shift in direction that was about to emerge. Again Clint suggests it was largely to keep the band interested in what they were doing. "We went to see Run DMC and The Beasty Boys at the Birmingham Odeon and we all thought it was brilliant, the best gig I'd seen in years. Really excit-ing. By this point we'd used up all the songs that we thought were substantial enough, so we were pretty much out of material. We needed time to get some new ideas, and we refused to put out anything substandard." Richard continues "It's just a different sort of thing, a move on to stop things getting boring. In Europe we got drunk in lots of discos and realised the only songs you can really dance to are ones with a great, strong beat. We thought we'd expand"[15] The transition was not an easy one however. The band were faced with a sometimes short-sighted response from the public as well as the major technical difficulties of the new set-up and sound. "When F1-11 came out we did a tour including four songs with taped drums. 'Beaver Patrol' was a cover of a band called The Wild Knights - Bobby Gillespie gave it to me and I thought it was a top song. So we did a cover of that, 'F1-11', 'Grebo Guru' and 'There is No Love Between Us Anymore' with the tape. The Birmingham gig was the best one of the tour, but the rest was absolutely appalling because we were messing about with the tape, then swapping live drums for the tape - it was a complete mish-mash. But we could have done it the old style and it would have been a great tour but that wouldn't have got us to where we wanted to go. We got slagged off no-end, and there's no two ways about it, the tour was really crap. This was all the more depressing because up to that point we'd been a really good live band."

"With the album, at first we thought we'd go for a mix of the two, so we went to the Fon Studio in Sheffield, run by Robert Gordon who had done a re-mix of 'F1-11' which we really liked. We demoed the album at Stanway Studios and in the meantime recorded another Peel session. We knew Gordon was good at the dance stuff and we knew we could do the guitar work. The sounds he started getting were brilliant - we knew straight away they wouldn't work on the old stuff. In the studio we came up with 'Intergalactic Love Mission', 'She's Surreal' and 'Hit The Hi-Tech Groove'. There is still something of a mish-mash on the album for me, because of 'Inside You', 'Evelyn' and 'U.B.L.U.D.' As a whole though it came together really well, and the sampling came very naturally. On 'She's Surreal' Gra had a bit from a Marc Bolan track which he looped and then Robert put a drum track behind it. Me and Gra then worked the vocal out. The guitar, I kid you not, Rich did in one take and it sounded brilliant. It's great when stuff works like that. "Of the change in direction, one critic wrote: "In a few months, the Poppies have changed dramatically. They are no longer old pub rockers from Brum but 20th century, hi-tech, mouthy gobshit bastards, stealing, thieving, sampling and cheating their way through the squalid history of pop." Clint was equally confident - " I'm not embarrassed by any of the records we've put out. I may not be into them now, but when we did them we thought they were brilliant. Probably in six months time we won't be able to stand this album. I think that's good."[16]

The continual ups and downs of their careers were again present on the album campaign. 'Beaver Patrol' got to No.75 but was heavily criticised for it's sexist connotations. Pete Paisley was not over-impressed: "Say it loud: PWEI's sexism, like the awful misogyny of so many rappers and hip-hoppers, stinks to high hell. Their boyish energy, all splay-legged ape stances and general falling over, nearly makes up for the infantile sexuality. But despite the distracting and often engaging gadding about, the dreggy elements are never far away. PWEI are basically an unkempt, idiotic New Order, high on hip hop and 'knockabout' comedy and not in the least afraid to let it all rip in one big trouser burp of a set."[17] Clint rejects this criticism of 'Beaver Patrol' as similar to trying to analyse Sid the Sexist. One reviewer at a sold-out gig (after a public mauling for the single) saw this as proof of the Poppies pedigree: "It is testament to the band's belief in themselves and the power of their music that they can come through the savaging they got for 'Beaver Patrol' and still manage to attract 1200 teenage fans as well as various managers and members of Krush, Sonic Youth, Big Black, The Jesus and Mary Chain, and Music of Life."[18]

On 3rd October the band got the front cover of NME - the album didn't chart at all. However, the band remember the tour as one of their best : "The tour was great - we did two nights at The Marquee and we had the whole set working on drum machine by now. We did the album tour in November and after Christmas we sold out the University of London to 1000 - we were well chuffed about that. Then after all that, we went to Europe on a really long six week tour. It was terrible, nobody was really interested and it just wasn't any fun, just gruelling. We did it anyway and came home. By that point it was time to start again because the album had gone as far as it could." Even so the band had survived that crucial period of change - "we'd got through that embryonic phase of 'F1-11' . It hindered us in that some people lost interest but we also got new fans. We've always thought that there's no point in staying the same, because people get bored and you yourself get bored. You've got to be creative, that's the whole point of being in a band. That tour as a whole was bloody good stuff."

It was on this tour that a Russian music critic, as a guest of NME, saw PWEI for the first time and was instantly converted. After having seen PIL and Public Enemy, he was far more impressed by the Poppies: "This band are brilliant. They have all the best elements of pop and have synthesised them into something new, tuneful and entertaining...they could have as much cultural impact in my country as The Beatles."[19] He consequently arranged four dates in the Soviet Union, one of the first 'indie' tours in that country. In a sense PWEI were probably the most unlikely musical ambassadors for Britain, particularly since their music was so clearly devoid of any political content. Once in Russia they did not talk politics but were clearly moved by the whole experience: "In a way we felt humble, because we came on and they went apeshit and I think they would have gone apeshit for any Western bands..you felt humbled by their reception so we felt a duty to entertain," said Adam. They found the whole music scene over there incredibly backward and had to politely reject offers of gig exchanges with sub-standard bands. For the "four Grebo Gorbyniks in their leather trousers , hangovers and crap haircuts" the culture shock was not only musical. A lack of basic items (particularly alcohol) surprised them as did Russian fashions - "It's like being a fourteen year old and your mum's bought you some awful clothes for your cousin's engagement party and there's no way you can get out of wearing it."[20] The whole tour added to PWEI's growing status as one of the leading bands of the British indie scene.

Back at home, by 1988 PWEI found themselves listening to more and more dance music, such as Bomb the Bass and Public Enemy, and just as the Ned's were aware of Manchester, the Poppies were unavoidably embroiled in this surge of club music. "We decided to demo a couple of ideas, which were 'Defcon 1' and 'Radio PWEI' back at Fon with Richard. 'Defcon 1' came out so good we decided to release it as a single." Clint said of this release "we've had a lot of trouble with beefburgers in the past. I think it's all some kind of global manipulation by Ronnie Macdonald. I keep having a nightmare where they 'phone us and

tell us they're using the song for their new commercial...shit, bang goes our hard-earned credibility." Um..Despite being ridiculed for mixing politics with McNuggets, Clint cites boredom again as a reason for the latest PWEI offering - "I'd just about reached saturation point singing about shagging birds, so I thought I'd better think of summat else quick."[21] On a live level "We did a couple of gigs to back up the release, at Birmingham Powerhaus supported by The Wonder Stuff, and The Astoria, both of which were sold out. I remember the Brum show because The Stuffies were about to sign to Polydor and they were waiting for 'Wish Away' to chart. 'Defcon 1' only got to about No.61 but we sold out these big dates anyway. We had established ourselves quite well by now in a way, although we've never had real hard followings like the Ned's and the Stuffies - probably no more than ten. In a way I'm glad because those bands get some hassles from that side of things sometimes, just hangers-on. At the time of these gigs we'd decided that we needed to move on from Chapter 22 - we were doing gigs like the Astoria and the same size as bands like All about Eve and we weren't on a major. So fairly quickly we got this deal sorted out with London Records. They signed us on the Friday, saw us sell out the Astoria on the Saturday, supported by The Wonder Stuff, and then they dropped us on the Monday, and to this day we don't know why, politics I suppose. We were so depressed." The official line from a London Records spokesman was "We did want to sign the band, but we changed our minds. The reasons are not simple and it is unfair to everyone involved to discuss them with the press." Clint remains sceptical of the whole affair "I doubt if he was actually there, it was the best show we'd ever done. Basically he lost his bottle, because what PWEI were doing was pretty diffrerent." By the time they signed they had had three other offers on the table - the band were clearly in the driving seat. Clint was less sure of their position but things soon changed again: "Fortunately Corda Marshall of RCA was at the Astoria and he thought we were great, but he knew we'd signed to London. As it happened his girlfriend at the time was the lady who'd signed us to RCA Publishing,and she told him the deal had fallen through. He came straight over and put us in the studio. We recorded 'Wake Up Time to Die', 'Can

You Dig It', 'Wise Up Sucker', 'Preaching to the Perverted', something like that, in two weeks in this studio in Wolverhampton. He liked it so we signed to RCA about two months after the London farce."

The band are at ease with RCA and have generally enjoyed good relations: "The record deal gives us a lot of freedom but we're always open - there's no point being pig-headed about it. They held back the album 'The PWEI Cure For Sanity' to create more demand - okay that's playing games maybe, but it's fair enough. At the end of the day there's the art of the song, but there's also the commercialism which is unavoidable. It's all steeped in street-cred about scruples and morals - bollocks, at the end of the day it' s just music and it's not worth getting worried about. If the band are happy with it then I don't think it's a problem. If we're comfortable with it then we'll do it - the people who moan are so narrow-minded anyway they're not worth bothering about."

Once again PWEI were to have major problems straight after a run of success - it was at this point that they were offered the Run DMC/Public Enemy tour. Ironically, The Sport for once appeared to have a modicom of foresight when it predicted hard times for PWEI: "Controversial grebo rockers PWEI seem to have finally bitten off more than they can chew..(by accepting)..an offer of the opening slot on the long- awaited Run DMC/Public Enemy/Derek B tour. British rap audiences are not renowned for sitting quietly through the warm-up sets for their heroes, so singer Clint and his band could well be in for a rough ride..."[22] Clint remembers how excited the band were at the prospect: "We were writing new stuff which was to make up the 'This Is The Day, This Is The Hour, This Is This' album. There were only two (big) dates in London and then they'd be doing thirty or so dates in massive venues all over Europe. We thought it would be great - as it was we got bottled off stage the first four gigs and came home. The problem was they had a real hardcore hiphop audience who just didn't like us. I think they thought we were taking the piss, I don't think it was a racist thing because even in Belgium there were mostly white audiences and they still hated us. Stephen Wells of the NME came on tour with us and after the gigs he interviewed the audience, who said they didn't like us because we used guitars. He suggested that 'Walk This Way' had guitars on it, but they replied that we still weren't real hip hop - they were very blind, very narrow-minded. The worst night was probably Brixton Academy - it was packed with about 5000 people and we went on stage to a blast from these hooters and whistles they have - it was the most intimidating experience of my life. As soon as we started they went fucking mad, and I don't mean in a good way. They threw everything they could find at us - bottles, umbrellas, burning paper, and we were showered with coins. Our roadie picked up about eight quid off the stage. We did our four songs and got off knowing full well that the next night we'd have to do it all again - bloody intimidating I can tell you. In Holland we didn't even finish the four songs. We started getting mad, so they gobbed at us and we gobbed back - it was going to end in one big fight. In the end we got kicked off the tour - so this thirty date tour had suddenly just disappeared. It was an incredibly depressing time. I've since heard that Run DMC would like to work with us again, but to be honest, I couldn't be arsed."

The band were now looking for their next single release. "We came home and started recording with Dave and Andy out of The Fine Young Cannibals, to do 'Can You Dig It' for a summer release. It took ages and we just didn't like it. As much as I like them two they were going to give us a hit single, which is great but not if you don't like the way it sounds - we've always known exactly what sound we've been looking for. That didn't really work - it took three weeks to do the single so our budget was through the roof. We'd wanted to work with the producer Flood but he wasn't available until after Christmas. So we started on the album with most of the stuff virtually ready - we worked solid for a month and then released 'Can You Dig It'." This provided the bands best chart success thus far; Richard cites an interesting analogy for the experience: "Listening to the radio that evening - not expecting the record to be in the charts, but hoping it was - was like Christmas morning; you hope you're gonna get Scalectrix but you open the present really carefully in case it isn't." The release was backed up once more by live dates, including a sell-out at The Town and Country Club, the groups largest gig to date. Almost predictably, in true PWEI tradition it was a disaster. "We came on, it was absolutely heaving, and launched into 'Defcon 1'. Half way through Adam's guitar packed in, I got hit on the head with a glass and lost my temper. The whole thing was really bad, probably the worst gig we've ever done. As it happened that week 'Can You Dig It' charted and the video was on Top of the Pops - it's always the same story." Reviewers saw the T&C date differently: "they were just brilliant , a perfect fusion of boyish rock fantasies and techno-brutal hip-hop realities. And funny too....Clint onstage is a cartoon sex-god, Jim Morrison escaped from an episode of Scooby Doo!..this is very possibly the best live band in Britain today..."[23] The album was finished and released by May. 'Wise Up Sucker' only reached No.41, but the band continued to get major press including a cover story in NME. The album itself charted at No.23, but the tour was surprisingly not a major success, with the band struggling to pull the crowds outside London.

Like Ned's and The Wonder Stuff, PWEI love playing Reading. " It's easier, more nerve-racking but less embarassing than small gigs. Two days after 35,000 at Reading, we played to thirty two people in West Palm Beach. We were back stage thinking how embarrassing, but in these situations we always say you can't blame the people that are here for the people that aren't. In the past I've adopted a real bolshie attitude like at Mega's Wine Bar when the gig lasted six minutes because I walked off stage since there were about two people there to see us. Adam went mad and rightly so because I dropped them right in it - and it's not fair on the people who have paid to see you. That night in Palm Beach we did an absolutely blistering set and three or four encores - absolutely great."

1989 saw the Poppies' first venture across the big lake - "it was brilliant going across the world and people there know all the words to some song you wrote in your bedroom in Stourbridge. Great. The album did pretty well over there, and we came back to start thinking again. It was then that we got the Australian tour - it was like 600-700 people every night thousands of miles from home, it was a brilliant feeling." Like the previous excursions, the

trip to Australia and New Zealand found the band in good PWEI-form. After finding one of the few non-dress restricted clubs in New Zealand, the band were later ejected for their loud rendition of a particular Hari Krishna favourite and generally over-rowdy behaviour. On a live television show Graham caused havoc by reading out the auto-cue in synch with the presenter. They also experienced their first major injury when Gra broke his leg on stage in Melbourne. "He came off stage and fell down the stairs - we went back on and did a couple of encores, no problem. We got up the next day and jumped on this flash private jet to go to a festival in Brisbane. By this time his leg was killing, so he went to hospital and came back in plaster. We built him this throne at the back of the stage and he sort of presided over the whole proceedings - it worked really well, went down a storm in fact. When we did Melbourne we hired a forklift truck and put strobes on it and he'd go up and down and the lights would be flashing - it was great. We did the same at the Marquee as well, and it worked a treat - we'd thought about pulling the gigs but as it turned out it became a big event. You just have to get on with it." The band's second visit to Australia was backed much more substantially by the record company. Partly due to this and partly as a result of PWEI's growing popularity, the band found themselves playing to crowds equal to or more than those in the UK - 1200 in Melbourne, 1000 in Sydney - a considerable achievement by anybody's standards. A similar response was waiting for them on their second American tour where audiences were now more used to the Poppies' sound.

The next album 'The PWEI Cure For Sanity' proved to be a real struggle to write. At first they tried to write co-operatively, by jamming ideas. Three months were spent trying to work something out, and looking back Clint sees it only as a highly unproductive and frustrating time. " All we got that did work was 'Cicciolina', ("the 'Papa's Got a Brand New Pigbag' of the late '80's dance boom."[24]) '88 Seconds', 'Axemen', all very embryonically, very sparse. We were listening to a lot a dance stuff and The Stone Roses and Jane's Addiction were coming through as well. So we decided to go our separate ways for a couple of months to work on our own - we've all got loads of gear by now so we can pretty well do stuff on our own. For example, when we rehearse we can record an eight track demo live and that gets things done very quickly. By splitting up for a while, we did 'Dance of the Mad', '88 Seconds', 'Nightmare at 20,000 Feet', 'X, Y + Zee', 'Psychosexual', and 'Rhubarb.' Those two months had worked. The pressure of forcing yourselves to write was just no good, it was like being in From Eden all over again. When you just go home, go down the pub and relax the ideas come naturally. Then we watched the World Cup which was a real laugh." The band also released the best football song of the year - 'Touched by the Hand of Cicciolina', and appeared on Top of the Pops with the lady herself.

The album was recorded at The Black Barn in Surrey, in two periods of three weeks. Even with the material already demoed, Clint says the band experienced a few teething problems. "The first thing we did was 'Dance of the Mad' - we were just mixing it as the next single and Gra lost all confidence in the chorus, this was three in the morning and we're like 'Oh my God!!!' Anyway I had a chorus from another track which didn't make it onto the album which fitted perfectly - that's how it works with writing. In between the two sessions we did two nights at The Institute in Birmingham, which was really great because sometimes you wonder if people are still into the band or not. Luckily it was packed."

The album kicked off with 'Cicciolina' charting at No.28 - PWEI have no problems with BBC1 or Top of the Pops. "I quite enjoy all that stuff. It can be a bit of a drag but as a rule it's a good laugh, 'cos the record company put you up in a top hotel and you can get pissed up at their expense. Also this time we went out with the Banshees and we got on really well which was brilliant 'cos that was one of our first bands - we all got legless together, great laugh. I don't see Top of the Pops as a compromise, it's our track and we perform it as we want to - I just always think of when we were playing at The Peacocks Club in Stourbridge as Wild and Wandering and just laugh."

The album however, was not well received by the critics - it didn't chart as well as the last one but sold better. That did not stop PWEI selling thousands of seats for the tour. Clint remains philosophical about the initial bad response: " Okay the reviews were bad but people still loved the band - our absence had built up expectations of our live show. The live reviews were considerably more positive: "Yes, the band can be penis-heads. Very easily, they've been practising for 20-plus years - and yes they do talk a load of poppiecock at times. Yet on stage that all becomes irrelevant when faced with the fact that PWEI are the best white dance band extant."[25] Clint is fairly immune to any criticism: "We were really happy with the album so let 'em slag us off - more people than ever are liking us now. We re-mixed 'X,Y + Zee' and it went in the charts mid-week at 21; when we went in at No.18 we had a massive party with all me mom and dad's mates 'round drinking loads of beer."

Similar success came with the fifth single from the album '92 Degrees Fahrenheit', the Poppies seventh top fifty hit. The popularity now enjoyed by the band was never more apparent than at Reading, when PWEI played third on the Friday night bill below Sonic Youth and Iggy Pop. Everett True was unusually generous in his Melody Maker review "they haven't one ounce of talent, wit or hope..they're as artistic as a fart in a painted bottle, unremittingly colourless and joyless and crap."[26]

The end of the year and opening of 1992 saw the band enter the studio to record their fourth album, their third on RCA. It also marked the arrival of Fuzz on drums replacing the often unpredictable Dr. Nightmare drum machine. The transition appears to have passed easily, as Fuzz explains: "They came up to me in a club and asked me if I was interested, probably because they didn`t know anybody else who would talk to them. They knew of me through other bands and various things I`d been involved in, but originally they only asked me to play the live shows. I think they must have liked me because after a while they thought they`d use me for the studio as well, probably to get their money`s worth. Coping at this level wasn`t too much to handle really because I`m basically a musical prostitute and have been involved in loads of stuff previously at all levels. I`m a reformed characetr now though.After two days I`d got used to them and it worked great - I really enjoyed it. The whole thing has been extremely pleasant and surprisingly easy to work in - their ideas seem to be ones that I like anyway, so there haven`t really been

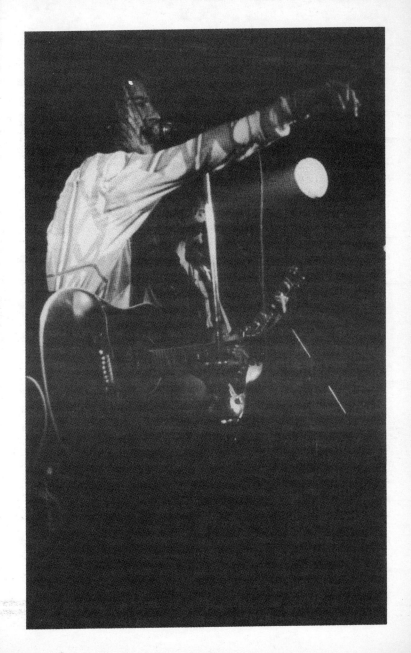

any difficulties at all." The new line up stormed into the charts at No. 17 with 'Karmadrome' in May, 1992. After a long lay off PWEI proved that they can hold their own with any band currently in Britain by playing five consecutive nights at The Marquee in London, four of which were sold out. Here the reviewers were rather more accomodating: "After a lengthy sabbatical..PWEI reclaim their reputation as an ass-kickin' live band, their rock/dance mayhem..as vibrant and infectious as ever, threatening to make your ears bleed. The Poppies are stars."[27] If further proof was needed that the Poppies are now as relevant and as popular as ever, it came with their rousing receptions at the Feile Festival in Ireland and also in Cardiff. Although some of the reviews for the second single from the album 'Bulletproof' were luke-warm, the chart position of No.17 justified the comment that "The Poppies have, on occasion, made pop music so wonderful that the gods themselves have wept with delight."[28]

Clint is very optimistic about the band's future - "we're now in a situation where people all over the world want to hear our next record - at least there's expectation for our new material. We want to get so much music into our stuff that it's not changing, it's just developing in context. It keeps it exciting for us as well." Adam feels this is a very healthy approach: "I think with out being conceited, we have been quite interesting. The name means we get used in newspaper headlines and most people have at least heard of us. But you have to have good tracks to back it up."[29] Of his own ambitions, Clint is rather more specific - "I'd really like one of those speedboats. It'd be brilliant to moor it somewhere like St. Tropez and hang out with girls with names like Plenty O'Toole."[30]

NED'S
ATOMIC
DUSTBIN

"One reviewer called us 'cider-crazed maniacs from some far field covered in dirt.' I wouldn't have minded but I'll have you know I had a wash the Monday before." RAT

CHAPTER TWO

Halesowen College of Further Education was the unsuspecting birthplace of Ned's Atomic Dustbin, where the rigours of academic tedium fuelled the hopes of four teenagers to be "..in a good band and play some gigs." Jonn, lead singer, continues: "We were in separate bands but were all completely sick to death of a lack of enthusiasm for what we were doing. We only knew of each other - I'd never spoken to Rat or Alex, but I think Mat had seen my old band a few times. I advertised for people on their enthusiasm only. What I got back was three bass players - Rat was a bass player at the time as well. Mat managed to get hold of Dan through a million-miles-an-hour metal guitarist called Wonga - none of us knew anything about Dan, except that he had probably been playing longer than any of us. It was really tentative for a while, because we didn't know if we all wanted to be in the same band. Then Dan couldn't decide whether he wanted to stay as a drummer or take up bass, so at one point we had four bass players!" With hindsight this 'musical quirk' of two bass players was an inspired choice of set-up, simulating the likes of Revenge, politico-rockers Delta 5, the bizarre The Logs and even the oft-praised Cure. At this stage however it was rather more out of necessity than choice. Mat remembers "I was down the pub and Jonn just walked up and said 'do you fancy being in a band?' The next week I bought a bass for £15 and found myself in a rehearsal room failing to play 'Wild Thing' and 'Knocking on Heaven's Door'. I'd never really considered it until Jonn asked me, and since I had nothing else to do except spend £1.50 a week on beer I said 'yes.' At the time people said the two basses thing was the worst idea ever but it's worked out fine." The unique Ned's sound was established at an early stage, as Alex recalls: "Jonn's advert just said 'Musicians wanted' - if you advertise for people influenced by a certain type of band then they'll inevitably end up sounding like those bands. As it is we all contribute with our respective tastes in music, strange as they are."

Fairly soon, they found the time needed for the band was a little more than most academic establishments would allow. With the benefit of hindsight, being thrown out of College was a relief; at the time it was less glamourous. "I remember shitting myself when we got kicked out of College and we didn't do anything for a month." Alex goes on: "You had to say 'Oh, I'm going to the dentist tomorrow,' and you were actually in Glasgow Barrowlands supporting The Wonder Stuff. When I got back all I could think of was the band. When we got thrown out we'd had no success so it was pretty scary."

Jonn's old band, 'The White Rabbits', had used a female vocalist alongside the Ned's lead man. "Because I liked the idea of that I suggested that we have a girl vocalist in the new band as well. They weren't too sure about it, but we did, probably because I was too pushy about it." Mat admits that at the time he was not confident enough of his own ability to argue - " I'd nearly had a fight with Alex because I thought I'd get the elbow since he could already play bass; so with the girl singer I just thought Jonn knew what he was doing because he'd been in a band before. I think it was a confidence thing - sort of a singing teddy bear. At this stage I'd just experienced my first jam - I didn't even know what one was until I got there, so I was hardly going to argue with Jonn. Once we had got together with all these people we started to rehearse hard." For eighteen months they trod the local circuits at such venues as The Mitre and Dudley JB's. Like the other two bands, this is where the Ned's learnt to appreciate the hard work involved in being a successful band - work which was rewarded by a loyal, albeit small local following. It was not easy though, as Mat recalls. "We kicked off at The Mitre, as everyone does, and after several months we'd progressed to this club called Rothschilds , which was distinctly dodgy. Half way through the set I broke a string - I was gutted because it had never happened before so I thought I'd broken my bass. I had no spares of course - the thought of spending £13 on guitar strings was simply horrifying. So there I was, swapping strings from my mates bass in the middle of a set - the crowd were not pleased. The next gig we did was at The Smiling Man which was even worse - Rat blew up his amp. Them were the days."

As well as playing host to the Ned's first gig, The Mitre pub also had several notable regulars amongst its smoke-laden wooden beams. One of these was Clint of PWEI. The normally quiet Alex plucked up the (Dutch) courage to ask the Poppie if he knew of a bass amplifier to replace his own "distinctly dodgy" set-up. Partly out of curiosity, and partly out of a protective instinct towards his expensive gear, Clint ventured upstairs to the function room. Jonn recalls: "Clint saw us and expected us to be dire - he was surprised, but we weren't brilliant. The music was not really the same. It was far more..not thrashy, but more driving, with real go-for-it drum beats, nothing dancy in there at all." "That first night I saw the Ned's they were bloody brilliant." says Clint, "I think that night I must have played 'Plug Me In' about fifty times when I got home." Such was his reaction that the Ned's consequently supported the Poppies for two gigs, at Coventry and Leicester Polytechics, albeit third on the bill in front of a very loyal PWEI crowd. Mat remembers those gigs as "...stunning. It was really great because the Poppies were a proper band. The gigs themselves were a nightmare because we didn't have a clue what we were doing. First we couldn't find the place and then when we got there it was like 'how fucking big is this?'. Up to that point we'd never played anywhere bigger than Wordsley Youth Centre. We got through it although there was hardly anybody there when we were on - there were a few who liked us which I found a bit overwhelming. I stood there all night scared stiff, hiding behind my Ride haircut."

The band impressed sufficiently enough to earn themselves a further three slots bolstering the Poppies, including one in London, the first time they had ventured to the capital. Jonn still rates one of these gigs, at the Manchester International, as one of his favourite nights with the band. At the Coventry Polytechnic gig were one of the Poppies engineers, Alex and Tank, brother to the Stuffies drummer Martin. "It was at the Coventry Polytechnic gig, that these two decided between them to try to help us out for a bit. Unfortunately Alex found that he hadn't got the time

because of his commitments with the Poppies, so Tank soon took over." Tank himself remembers that first taste of the Ned's: "When I first saw them supporting PWEI at Coventry Poly they were crap - I met Alex briefly, then I heard a tape of 'Plug Me In' and thought it was brilliant, so I went to see them again, in front of fifty people at The Mitre. They were spectacularly unorganised, and had no stage presence whatsoever. They went down well to their mates, but everybody else just stared on blankly. So I said I'd help them and then I got home and thought to myself 'What the hell have I said that for?' The next week I got us a support with The Wonder Stuff so I was a bit of a hero, but after that it's been all downhill really!"

This date was third on the bill at the Birmingham Hummingbird, as part of the 'Disco King Tour' - this was to be the last gig with the female vocalist, who did not prove to be consistent enough and so the band parted company with her. This was also 'the favour' which Tank was going to get from his brother, nothing else, which he now sees as beneficial: "It was useful, but we were terrible, although we seemed to go down okay." Jonn explains "We then took a while out to write some new songs and for me to work out what I was doing on all the old songs. Suddenly it all made sense...all the songs that had been clumsy before now worked because there was loads of space for melodies". Tank remembers the business side early on was not exactly lucrative: "We started off using a lot of money I didn't have, and also joined the Enterprise Allowance scheme. I'm not a manager and still aren't - I think berk's probably a better word! We did a lot of stuff off the back of loans from friends - Mat's aunt lent us money to buy a van for example."

At this time the Manchester scene was starting to explode; Jonn says "Some things come about that effect everything, all types of music. The fact that people started to dance to all this stuff must have effected our music and influenced it. Although we have always been set up as an anti-Manchester band and we were never really a baggy band, (none of that lark), the other side of it is that songs like 'Kill Your T.V' for example, are typical drum beats from Manchester and also from music like the Stuffies and PWEI. It just made so much more sense than beating out this

tedious 4-4 drums all the time." The band's characteristic rythmn changes also developed during this period. Mat says "we use a lot of tempo changes, changing things after about every four bars (because) if we play any longer than that we get bored. You can riff for ever but if the drums aren't there it just doesn't click."[1] Jonn says that "this and the business with the two basses was perfectly natural. It was never forced - our songs get together from an idea that is maybe two bars long. They play it and we then look for a chorus, a break or whatever. We put the pieces together, all of us. I don't write guitar lines because I'm not a guitarist, but we all contribute."

In the meantime, Mega City Four had seen the Ned's and liked them enough to proffer a support slot to Tank, with whom they were already familiar. "That worked out really well," says Jonn "because from that we got a great response, a good review in Sounds and most importantly perhaps, the Stuffies were there. This time Miles liked us (he saw them at The Mitre once and was not over-impressed). Tank approached them and they gave us the 'Hup' tour, an outrageous piece of good fortune on a load of levels. It was lucky that The Stuffies wanted a band of their own choosing, that they could get on with on the tour - they didn't want individual, unknown local bands third on the bill. We obviously weren't going to be any trouble." This tour went on to appear in front of over 25,000 people at major venues. Initially the Neds were followed by The Sandkings, and then for the second half of the tour by the now reformed Eat. With these dates people began to accuse and belittle the band by suggesting that they were milking the success of the two senior bands from the area, PWEI and The Wonder Stuff. Ned's react very defensively to such accusations, understandably, although they are realistic enough to admit that it was The Stuffies penchant for a local band (who would be easy to get on with), that gave them something of a headstart. Tank reacts angrily to such derisory comments however: "My brother didn't go out and buy the 60,000 albums that we sold in three days. The Ned's songs have done the real work. You don't sell out Kilburn National because your brother's in The Wonder Stuff. For the first six weeks I thought it would be great having Martin as a brother. But then it clicked that that would always be held against us. People thought that because of Martin we instantly got a tour, when in fact he said 'no, go and do it off your own bat,' which was fair enough (although I was upset at the time)." In many ways, supporting bands like The Wonder Stuff is ultimately harder since the standards are that much higher. Jonn argues "no matter what sort of music you play, if you play it badly then people won't like it." Dave Morris of The Work Shop Studio suggests "touring with The Wonder Stuff undoubtedly put them in the public eye, but they still had to go out there and do it. If they hadn't got it, then all the big name touring in the world isn't going to make people buy your records. If they'd been crap they would not have made it. You've still got to have something that the punters want. Take Stock, Aitken and Waterman for example - those kids don't buy Kylie to make the producers rich, they buy it because they like the music." Jim-Bob of Carter The Unstoppable Sex Machine is even more dismissive of such accusations: "I don't think they're a poor man's Wonder Stuff, they're actually better than The Wonder Stuff.."[2]

It was at this point that Tank remembers the Neds started to produce new material: "Two weeks prior to the Stuffies tour these songs appeared out of nowhere and they were brilliant. I went from thinking 'they're good' to 'they're better than anybody else' from my personal point of view. Now I was in a squat in Redditch and they'd suddenly written these great, but silly songs like 'Terminally Groovy' and 'Kill Your TV'. It was a really exciting time. Liverpool Royal Court on the 'Hup' tour was our first really successful gig. The doors opened at 7.30pm so people had had a nice quiet drink(!). The crowd went mad and the band really enjoyed it. We sold twenty two T-shirts and couldn't believe that people would spend some of their money on us - that was a real heart-warming experience."

Jonn remembers his apprehension at getting to know Miles: "I had to sleep with Miles after one gig, and I didn't really know him at all. There was nowhere to sleep so we were drawing straws to see who would share Miles' bed 'cos we were all so shy. To try to break the ice he rolled over and said 'Let's have a farting competition' and proceeded to break wind rampantly. I was so nervous I

couldn't fart for the first time in my life." Rat highlighted another
episode on the tour: "One night this chap was sleeping in the
same room as us. He rolled over in his sleeping bag and out flops
this glossy magazine. We all went 'Wey- hey!!' Anyway it was a
train-spotters magazine called 'Motive Monthly', a real disappointment."

Nevertheless, Jonn believes the band gained enormously in
many ways from this lengthy tour. "The people who watched The
Stuffies then became the core of our following, because they are
the sort of people who, if they like a band, they will follow them -
this is why the tour was so lucky for us. It was exactly the right
tour at the time, spot on." Prior to these dates they were not
exactly lively on stage; Tank remembers "They were great in their
own strange way, but at this stage they were absolutely stationary.
Rat rarely faced the crowd, Mat hid four feet behind the drum
kit. There was only Jonn who had the confidence to be natural
about it all. It's not until things happened that they got the confidence in themselves. Even later on, Rat didn't want us to release
a record at all because he just thought it just wouldn't sell - it
went straight in the Indie charts at No.2." During the tour there
were another incidents which all helped to boost the bands confidence: "We phoned Simon Williams (a music journalist) up and
he said 'Oh, I've heard of you lot, I've been trying to get in
touch.' We were so chuffed that somebody outside of our circle of
mates had actually heard of us."

In such an atmosphere, the Ned's began to develop their own
character and continued to earn loyal followers. "We learnt very
quickly that on a big stage you have to go for it," says Jonn, "..as
you become more and more at home on stage, you realise that
you have to shake your head around or do something." The practical considerations of a lengthy tour are invariably lost on an
eager punter -"clothes for the stage have to be practical, shirts
paper thin and horrible and shoes you can jump around in. The
rest of the lads wear T-shirts because they get very hot. It has to
look interesting - we want to be something worth looking at, but
it doesn't go as far as having a contrived image." The rest of the
band usually wear shorts, but Jonn still admits " I can't get my
head 'round 'em, with my legs they look stupid. You just have to

learn to entertain people. If you play fast music and just stand there then nobody will want to know." Their eagerness to put on a great live show is born, in Jonn's case out of fear - "Being booed off stage is something I've feared all my life." The tour was not all roses however; Tank remembers the legistics of the whole period were never easy: "The Wonder Stuff tour was a nightmare in many ways - we stretched people's hospitality to the limit. We used eleven different vans and ended up hiring one because all ours blew up. We actually missed one gig in Hull because the van had broken down. Still, we had our first press and sold some T-shirts on that tour."

Despite their close proximity to the Stuffies there is still a clear deference to their "big brother", a characteristic feature of the these three bands. It clearly didn't change Jonn's attitude towards Miles and Co. "Even being familiar with them didn't really make me see them any differently - I loved the band more at the end of the tour than I did at the start." Indeed, Jonn feels that on that first support tour they may have been an annoyance to the headliners. Having now headlined a tour themselves, they acknowledge that support bands can often be awkward, if like themselves, "they spend a whole tour asking questions - we were just trying to learn the trade really."

With these dates behind them the band were now beginning to emerge as one of the most exciting live bands in the country, but as yet they had not achieved any real acclaim in London. Christmas 1989 changed that, when the band supported the Poppies at The Marquee. The excellent reception provided them with a yardstick of their potential and a recognition of their growth since the days of The Mitre. The 'Hup' tour had seen the Ned's playing in front of large audiences - this was not considered enough however to launch their own headline tour, not yet. Thus the band set out on another support slot, this time going on before The Sears, on the so- called 'toilet tour' of venues in Britain in early '90. The band found however, that after the big stages of the 'Hup' tour, these much smaller venues were perhaps more difficult to play in some ways, but the whole performance, since they had learned to be active enough to cover a much larger stage, were "electrifying," and more enjoyable in many ways also.

"On a small stage it is far more realistic, and being closer to the punters means it's more of a shared experience." Mat prefers the smaller venue as "you have to be intimate, and it's a much nicer feeling." The band gradually began to steal the show from the headliners, and when the final date of the tour at the Marquee arrived, most of the audience were there to see Ned's.

It was during this year that the Neds had what Mat describes as "...our worst gig ever. It was at Santa Pod in Northamptonshire at a VW Beetle rally. Rose of Avalanche were playing, then us and then the Mega's. When we got there, there was this burger stall like the ones you see outside Villa Park, on a Saturday afternoon - that was the stage. We had a few followers down for the day so we felt okay about it. The problem was there were hundreds of Gazzas drinking gallons of beer - Rose of Avalanche got absolutely showered with stuff. We were due on next and I've never felt so intimidated in my life. As soon as we got on it started to rain and the crowd were having this massive fight, really violent I can tell you. Halfway through the set the security men started to lose control so Jonn was asked to calm the crowd down. Next he was asked to tell them to move away from the stage or we'd go off, and finally he was told to leg it. I've never seen anything like the mess after. The Mega's had their van smashed up and the site was just completely trashed." Rat found it all comical: "Santa Pod was more funny than anything else - at the end of the night there was blood all down the front of the barriers from these massive fights." This was not the only bad gig the band have had; Alex remembers two others which are particularly unworthy of note: "Mat's knob fell out at Leed's University, so he had to change his shorts in the middle of a gig. The worst gig was when we supported The Metal Gurus in Fulham Greyhound - we didn't get one single clap after any song. Not one. The crowd weren't very receptive at all thinking about it."

It was in January 1990 that Chapter 22 got involved. They provided much needed finance towards the cost of the tour and the band's first vinyl, 'The Ingredients E.P.' Tank felt the release was just about in time: "At this point, it was being compared to the buzz about the Banshees - they were massive and hadn't released a record. I thought that was a great comparison to be

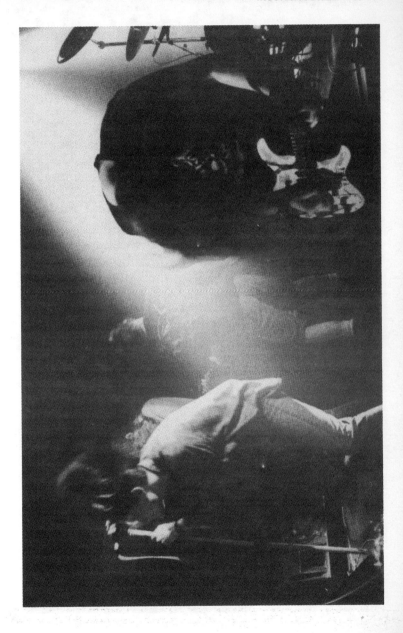

made. We wouldn't hang around any longer so we had to start releasing. As it was the final cut was great, but it had to be re-recorded because the first one was shit." Tank was very happy to be signed to the Birmingham label: "Chapter 22 - great label. They've nurtured so many good bands. Craig Jennings (Managing Director) sees things a lot earlier than most people, he's a very talented bloke. The problem we had was that he was being badly let down by distribution (Nine Mile Cartel). With 'Until You Find Out' we had a mid-week chart position of No.33, with the video on The Chart Show and all that - we thought we were raving. Anyway they ran out of records on the Wednesday - we were playing 900 plus capacity venues, and we were selling vinyl, it was just that people couldn't get hold of the single. I had people in Leicester, Liverpool, even London hassling us because they couldn't get it. HMV in London had one copy." It was frustrating in the extreme when the single consequently ended the week at No.54. This was one of the major reasons why Ned's eventually moved to Sony, to gain access to wider distribution.

'The Ingredients E.P.' was backed by the band's first headline tour of the country, again in what they endearingly call 'the toilet venues' of the country. Jonn was not prepared to become complacent however - "...you are still talking of only about sixty people at smaller venues - that is not enough to sit back on, even with the six hundred or so we got in London." By now the band were developing a hard-core live following, which in their eyes is far more important than vinyl success, in order to get the band established in Jonn's view. It also gives the band greater chance of a reasonably long career - "the point is that if you build a following early on, by constantly gigging, and then your second thought is to bring out a record, then those people are far more permanent . If you release a record with all its hype you don't sell out a tour. The gigs will be full of twelve year olds who will be bored in a year." The release of the E.P. and tour was then followed by a support slot on the Jesus Jones 'Real, Real, Real' tour, in May and June of 1990, as the main support band. By now the music and the infamous T-shirts were achieving considerable notoriety: "The Jesus Jones tour was only six dates - we out-sold them on

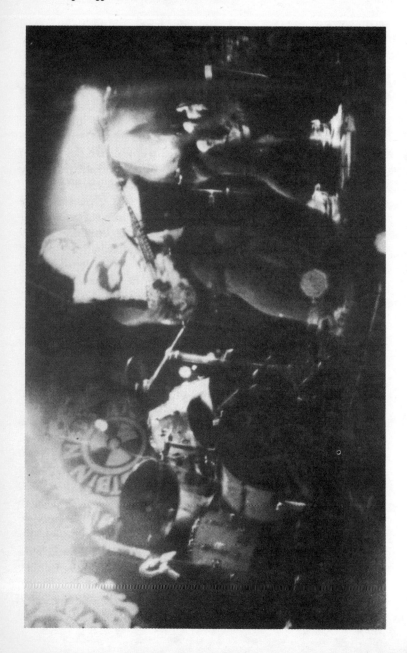

merchandise but they took it like men, right on the chin." This was followed by the band's second single 'Kill your Television', which was also promoted with a small tour in August. At the time this served to reinforce the band's following and to crystallise suspiscions that Ned's could soon threaten the charts. Tank remembers "We sold out Sheffield Lead Mill - our first sell-out, that was dead exciting. That gig was the first time we started to take the piss with the merchandise."

One of the highlights of 1990 for the band was the Reading Festival which was to prove to be "..a milestone saying 'we've arrived.'" It was 12 noon on a wet Saturday afternoon, and the day was only one band old - a typical apathetic early day festival scenario. Except for one thing - there were 30,000 people in the crowd waiting to see Ned's. Indeed, such was the anticipation about the band that the promoters deemed it necessary to put on another act first, otherwise they would have had the farcical situation of having thousands turn up to see the very first band on. Jonn astutely denounces the popular misconception that to play in front of 30 or 300 is the same as 30,000 as "bollocks", after having felt sick just before taking to the stage. Mat is reluctant to play the Festival again, because it was such a good gig - "Reading was the most acute experience I've ever had. I looked out from behind the curtain and my stomach just went on holiday. I walked on stage and shot straight up to the ceiling, and didn't come down until we'd finished. As I walked off stage I nearly fainted, I just kept thinking 'we did it, we did it'. Up until we went on we thought it was all some extravagant joke Tank was playing on us - he'd maybe got hold of some backstage passes and just maybe put all our gear on the stage for a laugh to scare us. The feeling was unbelievable, more so because some people wondered why we were on the bill at all and we went on and kicked some ass." Jonn agrees - "we got such a buzz from Reading it was outrageous. Afterwards we felt that anything was possible. The crowd just went completely bananas." Tank says "Reading - what a week. We hyped ourselves so much for that. It sort of confirmed a load of suspicions. We did a short set and made a great impression - you've never seen us so shit-scared." And finally Rat: "Reading was great but one reviewer called us 'cider-crazed manacs

from some far field covered in dirt.' I'll have you know I had a wash the Monday before."

Their third release was 'Until You Find Out', in October of 1990. In the manner of all of their previous releases the single was backed up by a comprehensive tour, this time sold out every night, headlining at much bigger venues. The shows in London, Birmingham and Manchester were sold out to crowds of between 1000 and 1500, whilst even the smaller suburban dates attracted audiences of on average 600 - "by this stage it was getting out of control almost." In November the band went to Holland to play a mini tour, which was recorded on Super 8 and constitutes a major part of the now hugely successful video 'Nothing Is Cool'. The series of dates abroad served to remind the band of their more humble beginnings, and according to Tank, was the ideal antidote to any complacency : "If you go to a venue and 1000 people are shouting and going wild, you get used to it. In Holland there were usually no more than 80 people and 79 had never heard of you, so we had to win people over again - it was great for that reason alone. We were just starting to get a bit cocky so it put us back to the bottom of the ladder again." The band also did three dates in Ireland and appeared to take to the Shamrock Isle. Tank remembers it for the native hospitality: "I tried to catch a cab in rainy Dublin at three in the morning on my birthday - this bloke picked me up and then these other people as well, who proceeded to offer me a bed for the night - great place." The sound engineer Si, had a less fortunate experience - "We set this PA on fire in Ireland - the Drogheda Boxing Club, which as you know, springs to mind on the list of popular venues. The PA was smaller than me, and stuck on this table. We were supposed to be doing a fifteen song set and Si just got a pen and crossed out all but the last three - it was impossible."

This excursion was followed by two sessions on Mark Goodier's and then John Peel's show. These proved to be ideal opportunities to demo the album, and to record for the first time material that had been played for two years live, without ever actually being recorded. Tracks included in these sessions were 'Selfish','Cut Up', 'Throwing Things', 'Nothing Like', 'You' and 'What Gives My Son'. The single 'Happy' and 'Capital Letters'

were not even written until later; indeed, 'Less than Useful' was written in the studio whilst recording the album.

The band's first taste of touring Europe was not a wholly enjoyble one: "In Germany we seemed to play nothing but shit-holes. You drive seventeen hours to a thousand seater venue and when you get there 120 people turn up because the promoter's done no posters and no advertising. Nightmare. After playing to 2000 people we went to a club in Munich and the power cut off. That reminded me of Luton 'Switch off ' Club many moons ago." Tank continues "We played in Belgium one day and then the south of Germany the next day - look that up on a map, it'a beast of a journey. But when you're on that budget you just have to play the gigs. The one gig was at a place for 1200 or so, and 100 turned up because The Pet Shop Boy's were playing a foot-ball stadium down the road on the same night. What sort of pro-motion is that? Brainless. That was one of the worst gigs we ever did."

The year 1990 culminated in a triumphant double sell-out of the London Astoria and Wolverhampton Civic. All the band felt this was a perfect end to a very productive year, and was particu-larly enjoyable because it was something of a home-coming. "Wolverhampton Civic became an event rather than a gig. It was the best atmosphere and we were worried it wouldn't sell out." In fact such was the demand for tickets that touts were selling them for £60 a piece. Alex felt it finally silenced all their critics and expressed this rather poetically: "We pissed in their crisp packets tonight..Standing on stage, looking out for the first time I thought 'We deserve this.' " Hugely popular they might be, but NME noted how they still appeared to have avoided the star trap, despite their success: "Ned's bassist Alex arrives in the band's dressing room only to be scolded by his mum: 'Look at the mess in here...it's just like your bedroom.' Brilliant."[3]

Their position in the relationship with Sony is very strong - Jonn says that through their own Furtive Label "we put this great big footprint that says what we can do. Basically we can record what we like, when we like, wherever and with whoever we want to, on whatever budget we feel is necessary (within reason). We also choose the sleeve, in fact my girlfriend designs most of the

sleeves and one of the following did the sleeve for the video and a lot of the T-shirts - it's that close to home. We also decide which singles are going to be released from that album." Mat goes on "nobody, including the record company has got anything to do with our t-shirts. We control the whole show - that was so important to keep us out of debt in the early days." In effect they are on their own label, Furtive, but backed by a major label - "they can distribute our records better than any other record company." Also the band have an independent Press Officer, and an independent Plugger who are employed by the band and not by Sony. The only flaw, if it is one, in the deal is that Sony are allowed by one clause to 'persuade' the band to do it their way - they cannot make them but it has proved to be "annoying" says Jonn. "They'll even go ahead and do something and wait for you to notice - shop dislays was a typical example where we didn't stop them in time. They put up displays that we didn't approve of, we hated 'em, they were really poxy. Stickers on the records also annoyed us because the 'includes the hit single' type suggests there are two good songs and eleven dead ones." Nevertheless, Jonn is not about to bite the hand that feeds him - he sympathises with bands who have a less independent deal " With the annoyance that these few things have caused, I can't imagine the hassle and damage they could do to some bands. At the end of the day that major record company is more orientated about money than anything else. That's why I feel so secure with our deal because it's so water-tight, that it protects us from all that lark. The lucky thing with us was that we'd achieved so much doing it our way already. The only reason a label of that size are interested is because they think 'Christ, this band are selling records,' that's it."

The raised eyebrows of many people when they find out who Ned's are signed to is proof that the band give the label a distinct credibilty, and helps them to move away from their muchmaligned 'Deacon Blue' image. For their trouble they get a band who are prepared to work continually and effectively do all the work that they, as a record company, would normally have to do. Thus the No.1 Indie single band could then seriously threaten the charts with all the national advertising and distribution of a major - the entrance of 'Happy' at No.16 was a total vindication of the label's decision to enter into such an apparently one-sided deal. With all of their bands they are in it for money and to make their names the biggest band in the world. Such ruthless capitalism does not daunt the band however - "we don't want to be the biggest band in the world this year, next year,...ever" says Jonn.

On the subject of their signing to a major, it is clear that Tank was not prepared to lose the independent nature of the band, partly because he had heard several horror stories of band manipulation by the record companies. "We signed after loads of A&R men had been chasing us 'round the country. We decided that we had to maintain control so we created our own Furtive Label. We felt that if we went swanking around on a major label like you owned the place, you would lose the loyalty of your following, people would get pissed off in ten seconds. So I said 'I've got a label and Ned's are the only band on that label - if you want them you'll have to have the label.' " His decision to maintain independence was soon vindicated: "With the formatting they wanted us to do five versions on the single ('Happy'). I was having none of this - comical really, because there I am telling Muff Winwood, (who's twice my age and has literally done everything), that I've got a better idea than him. I mean he trusted us with it - we were selling loads of tickets for major venues. So I said 'If this fails then we'll talk about it again, and you can format me to death. Muff has been in big groups, produced big groups, he's certainly no fuckwit. Some people in the business tell you what to do and they've never done a real tour or any hard gigging in their life. So he knows where he's at, but I knew we could do it our way. Our singles have no formats and no bullshit around them." ('Happy' charted as the second highest new entry for that week.)

In the space of twelve months the Ned's had established themselves as one of the most talked about acts in the country - " It's weird now" says Alex " that a year ago we were telling people to come to our gigs and now we're telling them not to because they won't get in." The Yuletide period saw them enter the studio to record their much awaited debut album. The band had still not achieved mainstream recognition in the form of chart success - that was soon to change however with the release of their fourth

single ' Happy', despite expectations from the band that "..it might go in at the lower end of the 30's". Tank recalls: " We were in Hull Tower Ball Room at the time. We were told about an hour before and all thought it was a lie - we were going wild in this service station when we heard the prediction. In Hull we were surrounded by all our crew and all our favourite people - it was great. The highest bet was No.24 (me) so we were well chuffed - out came the champagne! The album charting didn't seem so exciting after that." Although its chart life was relatively brief, its impact was enough to focus attention on the Ned's through extra press and a debut Top of the Pops appearance. Again this success was the result of hard touring, with a lengthy series of dates to coincide with the release - the band are clearly not prepared to be successful in abstentia.

Once again, this tour provided it's share of incidents. Rat remembers in Bradford ".. me and Alex playing football with this horrible kitten that had pissed in his sleeping bag." Alex continues: "This chap said we could stay at his place and it was the worst house I've ever seen - there were so many cats everywhere." Students are worse than incontinent cats as far as Jonn is concerned - he has clearly mused on the matter - "The reason that students have no cutlery is because it's all under their settees; that's when you get that particularly green cup of coffee that you can't turn down." Dan goes on: "In Sunderland there were seven of us, and these little nippers started chucking glasses at us and bricks and stuff like that." The tour also had its fair share of great gigs - "Glasgow Barrowlands is a great place to gig, there's something about it. The Scottish are so into their music and they went bananas. That night we had to sleep in the venue, and we got told off for skate-boarding on the dance floor - after there had been 2000 people stomping on it an hour earlier!" "University of London was a great gig as well. We rehearsed some encores with Mega City Four, so we were all on stage except Dan. He was chuffed because it was the first time he had ever seen us live!"

More considerable success was to come with the release on April 1st of the album "God Fodder". Again the band were 'surprised' to see it enter the album charts at No.4 (the album went silver - 60,000 copies - in three days). This time the tour was to

be their biggest and most comprehensive. The dates in Britain, the US and Japan reflect the bands rocketing popularity and also the record companies eagerness to transpose this success onto a world level as soon as possible. Indeed such is the extent of the tour that the proposed Australian leg had to be cancelled, simply because the legistics were too complex. Closer to home, The Town and Country and Kilburn National dates of that tour sold out their respective venues quicker than any band up to that time in the year. Mat however did not enjoy the home leg of the album tour - "I picked up a couple of injuries and never really got into it. Normally after a few days your body gets wound up and into it, but I never really did. Everybody else was really motoring but I just never got any momentum." There is perhaps particular interest in the bands growing following in Japan, currently the prime territory for Jesus Jones. Jonn says "In Japan we are causing a bit of a scam, I think. The punters over there seem to be very easily influenced and the press are almost fanatical - on the British leg of the album tour we had a recently arrived Japanese journalist every three days. We'll go over and do four dates in small venues to give them a taster, then we'll go back and do it properly."

The bands' enormous popularity was confirmed with their second on the bill apperance at Reading '91: "It wasn't as good as the year before but I expected that. We had a lot of sweat to get on the bill but I think we totally justified it." Further major success awaited the release of the single 'Trust' in September 1991, when they achieved their second Top 40 hit with an accompanying video spoof of the sixties American programe The Banana Splits; it was now apparent that Ned's had established themselves as very serious and long term chart contenders.

Once again the band launched into a gruelling worldwide series of dates covering America, Japan and Australia, most notably supporting Jesus Jones in the USA, where Mike Edwards' band had acheived a No.1 hit with 'Right Here, Right Now'. Mat explains: "Club Metro was a brilliant gig - the New Music Seminar was great as well except that there were only about 30 punters in there and the restwere just music biz standing around. The dates with Jesus Jones were superb because of their Billboard success - it was quite strange because we'd do a series of gigs and the album sales would jump by 13,000, especially since MTV took a really keen interest as well . Each time we go back to the USA the response seems to get better and better." Nevertheless the Ned's were tiring of touring by now and appeared in some of the music press as rather dejected and weary. Jonn became paranoid about flying, all of them succumbed to various strains of pneumonia, abscesses, colds, sore throats and so on. Mat hated the boredom most: "On tour I just smoke and smoke - I did stop for three months but as soon as we go on the road I start up again because there's nothing else to do." Jonn had a more worrying problem - "I came very close at times to jumping on Mat's bones because he wears sandalwood, the same scent as my girlfriend. I could quite easily have snogged him." Fears were also voiced about the unsettling effect of so much touring: "This time last year I knew I came from Stourbridge. Now I don't know where the fuck I come from, I don't know what I'm doing."[4] "1991 was a haze - loads of people wanted us all over the place all the time and we were working non-stop. Now we've learnt to moderate things, it's easier to control what's going on and enjoy it more."

It was not all downhill however, as Mat recalls: :"We were doing an interview on KRock Radio and Rat said 'We're having this party and anybody who's interested can come down as long as you bring some beers.' I'd gone to see a gig in Hollywood so when I got back there were about three hundred peole at our hotel, lying all over the place, and the swimming pool was absolutely full of beer cans. The manager of the hotel was not very pleased - it was a right old knees-up. Also, the last time we were in America we stopped off in Chicago for a few days where it was about minus 50 degrees. We did some stuff with Paul Raven, ex-Killing Joke, and that sounded really good - at the time we had to leave so he mixed it. It didn't turn out as we thought, it was very good but it was nothing new, nothing that we hadn't done before. Also on that day I was in one of my 'I hate rock stars' moods and I had to go to the airport. As I came outside the lads had hired two massive white stretch limo's just to piss me off. At first I wouldn't get in but when we did the driver was a superb bloke and let us ransack the drinks cabinet for free, so it turned out alright in the end."

Japan held a certain fascination for some of the band, where 'Nedsomania' saw tickets selling weeks in advance. "Japan was great - the language barrier shields you from the culture shock because you don't know what's going on - a tour environment is so isolated anyway. As for the crowds being quiet - they all went absolutley fucking mental. Unbelieveble. Maybe other bands have a more cerebral Japanese audience. Also we have a certain number of people who go to every gig and get the crowd really going. We've got this bloke who works for us over there called Kondi who is more enthusiastic about the band than any of us were, are or ever will be. He works so hard at it it's incredible. He comes over here to see us and he'll buy 25 shirts three nights in a row, so Tank will be saying 'Look, I'll give them to you' but he'll insist on paying for them."

After a lightning tour of Britain in December when the band were as well received as ever, the Ned's began serious work on the much-awaited second album, punctuated by more overseas dates including some very succesful shows in Australia, a Finsbury Park appearance behind The Cult, and an Alternative Aids Awareness gig to coincide with the Wembley Freddie Mercury tribute. After some problems, Mat is very happy with the way the album has turned out: "We'd spent a long time writing the album; we decided to do the recording in three sessions. It was a brilliant way of working because it keeps you really fresh - also at that time we were all really in to it. There had been pressure with it but that was mainly from ourselves because we were aware that it was a year since we'd released a record. We ended up with ten songs ready and couldn't for the life of us write any more. We would argue and tempers were flaring from the tension. Then one day we just said 'That's it, there'll only be ten songs on the album, it's finished, we'll come in tomorrow and rehearse.' The next day we came in, the pressure to write had totally vanished and suddenly we came up with the rest of the album, no problem. That's what happens when you hassle yourslf, it goes nowhere. You have to take it easy."

"Now that the album is finished I'm really pleased with it. There are some great songs in there and I really enjoyed making it, and working with the outside producer Andy Wallace, who is

such a nice geezer and a briliant producer. The whole thing sounds a lot more focussed, a lot deeper, more complete. 'God Fodder' wasn't a lot of fun to make and we weren't very comfortable in the studio, whereas with this album it has to do well, there was a challenge and now I think it probably deserves to do well because we've invested a lot of time and effort into it. There's a lot of shit being released at the moment and I just think this is much better. There's also the element that it is our job and because 'God Fodder' took off so quickly it was almost like an unexpected bonus, whereas now it's our job. In a way I'm more concerned about what we can do on the third album than the world tour for this second one, because I know we can produce the goods live; I'd love to start writing again straight away if I could. As long as we keep making good records and enjoying what we're doing then we'll be fine, because the following are far too intelligent to be swayed by a music paper who wake up one day and decide to start slagging us off."

Manager Tank remains philosophical about the band's success - "It'll be interesting to see how long we can last - if we keep writing good songs then we should be okay... As Vanilla Ice said 'You're not a star until you've sold four platinum albums'... thanks Vanilla."

THE
WONDER
STUFF

*"It used to sound great in the back of my Dad's
Marina van..."*

Martin

CHAPTER THREE

It all started when a 16 year old Miles Hunt placed an advert in a local newspaper, and arranged to meet Malcolm Treece and Chris Fradgeley in Dudley: "I was a drummer in those days and I'd never worked with anybody outside of the kids in our village, so meeting these two characters in a pub car park was quite an ordeal. On the way, my old man said that he would stick around for ten minutes while we jammed, and if I didn't like it I was to give him a nod and he'd make an excuse so we could leave. When we were unloading the gear I said to Chris 'Has Malc got any effects?' at which point Malc turned round with this bloody great big board full of flangers and effects everywhere! When I saw all that I think I just had to be in. As it was we went inside and jammed around and after five minutes my dad could see it was good so he gave ME the nod and left."

Once Clint and Adam had joined, 'From Eden' got on with the business of playing the local circuits. However, despite a degree of success, Miles' departure was soon followed by that of Malcom and Chris. Malc continues: " It came to the stage where me and Chris wanted to do something a bit more serious and they wanted to do stuff a bit more Peely. We were into bands like Bryan Adams and King, whilst Clint and Ad were into The Three Johns and The Shop Assistants. It was just no good." Miles recalls the success of 'Wild and Wandering', later Pop Will Eat Itself, and the effect it had on him and Malc: "We watched it all and loved it, but we weren't doing anything about it. I'd watched Clint playing guitar and singing and I'd always wrote my own little songs, so when I heard Malc was looking for a singer I thought I'd give it a go."

"We'd done a few things" continues Malc, "but all pretty bad. We had various line-ups with names like The Hunger, These

Ashes, nothing any good. Then Miles phoned me up and asked to have a go at singing. We'd heard there was a drummer called Martin Gilks who had left The Mighty Lemon Drops so he joined as well. Chris wasn't very keen on the stuff we began doing so he left - now all we needed a bass player." For a while Rich Poppie filled in on bass, but it wasn't long before a friend, Bob Jones, was recruited, albeit on a fairly informal arrangement, and The Wonder Stuff was born. Miles was enthusiastic but cautious about leaving the relative safety of the drum kit: "I didn't know how I was going to react to another drummer, and I wasn't very confident of my guitar playing. Anyway, I had a couple of tunes with a few words and choruses, one of which was 'The Potato Song,' where we used to sing 'Our lives are like potatoes' - I don't remember if those were the actual words but people would always listen and ask 'Is he saying potato??' From the start it stood out from all the other bands we'd been in - we had loads of melodies and space for everything. With 'From Eden' we'd rarely had that - we'd just get riffs and bang along to it and say 'Clint do something with it!' "

Rehearsing initially in Miles' kitchen, The Wonder Stuff soon had a small set knocked into shape. Malcolm remembers hearing one song in particular for the first time: "I was with Bob and we were really late for this rehearsal. When I got there all I could hear was this bloody racket going 'P-P-P-Poison, P-P-P-Poison....' I thought 'This is great,' I couldn't hear any tune or anything like that but it sounded bloody great. We rehearsed these songs three nights in the week before our first gig, as well as an hour in the afternoon before the show - we went down to JB's in Dudley, and supported a band called 'Russian Roulette' with an half hour set including 'Red Berry Joy Town', 'She's the Rain' and 'Wonderful Day'."

"I was really excited about this new band," continues Miles "so I gave a tape to Mark Morris from Balaam and The Angel, who were the biggest band in the area at that time. He introduced me to Les Johnson, a local promoter, who had a listen to our tape, loved it and came to see us support The Poppies at Stourbridge Town Hall. He became involved, along with Dave Alldridge (who had also been at the Stourbridge gig) and things

immediately began to pick up". Dave Travis, a local promoter who arranged many of the early Wonder Stuff and PWEI gigs remembers receiving his first tape of the band - " I get hundreds of tapes thrown my way and this one was simply the best I'd heard in a very long time. As a band they were always ready to gig and always did the business. On one occasion they were up to support Half Man Half Biscuit, who unfortunately split up three days before the gig. We couldn't pull the gig so we let the Stuffies go on anyway - they went down great, and it was only a quid! At the time there weren't many good bands about so these two (The Wonder Stuff and PWEI) really stood out - I was always keen to put them on. They supported the Poppies at the Irish Centre in March '87 - a year later we had to cancel a Burberry's gig because they were simply too big to play there anymore." Les and Dave then suggested that the band record what they felt was a good single. Miles explains: "So we did these four tracks - the first attempt was absolutely awful and it got worse. The whole recording was absolutely rubbish. Les and Dave simply couldn't afford to pay for another session, so Bob said he'd put the money up because he'd just had a win on the pools. We knew of The Barn Studio in Warwickshire, which the Poppies had used for 'Oh Grebo I Think I Love You' so we went down there and recorded our first single, 'Wonderful Day E.P.'" Even with this vested interest, it was still not clear as to whether Bob Jones would stick around for as long as he did - he was continually on the move.

There were a thousand copies of the first single pressed - 500 were sold in shops in the Midlands and the remainder were given away, including a number which went to a few choice journalists. Polygra were interested enough to offer the band a publishing deal on the basis of this release, in the summer of 1987. With this more substantial backing, the band now had to choose their second single, as Miles recalls: "We'd decided 'A Wish Away' would be a good second single - we recorded a version on Clint's little Portastudio at home, which gave it a real Byrds feel. Unfortunately, however, it proved almost impossible to reproduce this in the studio - when we came round to the album version for example, it took five attempts, which is very unusual for us as we often bang stuff down in one take. That original portastudio version used to sound brilliant in the back of Martin's Dad's Marina van; in the main studio we got lost amongst footsteps and echoes and loads of effects - it was awful."

It was during this time that the band began to enjoy the jet-set life of the true pop star, as Martin continues: "That Marina Van was great. One night Dave phones up and says 'If you can get to Northampton by 8 o'clock you've got a gig supporting The Fall.' We were at Dave's house in Birmingham, the gear was at Stourbridge, and I had to get this van from Wolverhampton then over to Northampton, all by 8 o'clock. We were doing quite well until the distributor cap broke - it was held on by one piece of wire. It took us about three hours in the end so when we turned up at 9 we thought there was no chance of them letting us go on." Malcolm took care of the band introductions: "I walked into the foyer and says 'I'm looking for John Lennon' and this geezer says 'Well I'm John Lennard, will that do? Get on quick.' " Miles carries on "This guy sorted our guitars out for us, slaps a four pack into our hands and says 'Get on!!' Malc had to borrow a guitar strap so his guitar was up round his chin. When we went on the curtains were closed so we were messing about with the gear and making a complete racket. Suddenly the curtain goes back and everyone thinks it's The Fall so they go 'YEAH!!!', then they see us and go 'Oh dear.'"

Early Relations with Polygram, the publishing company, were infamously strained at times. Martin remembers how Miles instantly hit it off with the executives: "I remember him sitting there in the first meeting with all the Armani suits, and he's going on about posters saying how we don't ever want to do fly posters because they just don't work. So they said 'Well, what do you want to do? ' and he replied 'Well, I know what we don't want to do - be like that band 'Cactus World Fuckin News,' and we proceeded to slag them off until this dejected executive guy eventually says 'I signed Cactus World News.' In another instance, they nearly lost the whole deal itself, as Martin recalls: "We were at the Marquee, after a gig, drunk. Dave Alldridge, the manager who always kept us in order was in France; Les Johnson, the other manager was usually as out of order as us. This guy from Polygra was going on to me about signing us, even though we hadn't actually signed at that point. So I said "So would the deal still be on if I poured this pint of beer over you?' to which he replied 'THE DEAL WOULD BE OFF!!' So of course I had to chuck this whole pint of beer over him, as you do. He went absolutely mad. Later on we went over and said 'You ain't pissed off are you?' and this guy says 'Pissed off, I'M ABSOLUTELY BLOODY FURIOUS!!!' We humiliated him in front of half the record industry, and he threatened to drop the whole deal. He never did though."

Having finally decided on 'Unbearable' as the second single, in December 1987, things really started to accelerate. Dave Morris of The Work Shop Studio remembers that at this stage there was a noticeable edge to The Wonder Stuff: "I was aware when they came in that they had something that a lot of bands didn't have. The songwriting and the whole approach to everything was different, very positive. They'd demo a song and if it didn't work they would come up with another song - they never tried to re-work songs that weren't happening. 'Unbearable' was an instant two and a half minute pop song. There was a real freshness from these three minute pop songs which arguably hadn't been done properly since the sixties. It seems to me that The Wonder Stuff had and still have no trouble writing classic pop songs." The press were equally enthusiastic about the release; the NME said "on the strength of 'Unbearable', I'd say The Wonder Stuff were this year's great undiscovered band and next year they'll be mega." Record Mirror were equally enthusiastic: "Unbearable: the standout single of the year...huge, fat rascal guitars and a bitter-sweet lyric."[1] At the band's first London gig, in the winter of 1987, Dingwalls was heaving with masses of A&R men, all eager to experience the much-talked about new band. Andy Strickland of Record Mirror was there and recalls "I knew they were longhairs and possessed a crazy beast of a bassist. I hoped they'd overcome the oft-cited nerves many young bands suffer when first playing the capital. Miles, Malc, Rob and Martin strode onto the stage and proceeded to slay the audience with the most ferocious pop outburst I'd heard in years. Song after song of raunchy, ringing, ridiculously catchy noise topped off with Miles' flowing locks, cocky sucked-in cheeks - caressing his semi-

acoustic while Malc - a teenage Francis Rossi lookalike - hammered out skull-splitting noises from those silver strings. It was perfect!"[2] Such reviews were not isolated as The Wonder Stuff continued to cause a stir with their live performances.

The band were still watching and learning from Pop Will Eat Itself, but soon events began to speed up even more, to the extent hat they leapfrogged past the stage of doing hundreds of small town gigs in the back of vans. 'Unbearable' was used as part of the soundtrack for a Dan Ackroyd and Steve Martin film whilst back at home a serious A&R chase was beginning to develop which followed the band around the country. The Hedd label, a subsidiary of Virgin, offered them a tour with Big Country in return for signing to them. Miles continues "By this stage we knew full well that we were going to sign to Polydor, but we didn't tell them that. Hedd was run by The Cult's Management, and at one particular meeting Ian Astbury stuck his head round the door and said 'Have you got a light?' It was so obvious that he'd just been wheeled in to impress us so that we'd go 'Fucking hell it's IanAstbury!!!'. Anyway we went ' Fucking hell it's Ian Astbury!!!'. But it didn't convince us. When they found out about Polydor, we literally just left the tour, straight down to London and got bevvied up." The tour itself was enjoyed-Martin particularly liked the gig at Newcastle Mayfair: "It was a classic. The crowd went absolutely mental for the first time for us ever. We presumed they thought we were Big Country but they knew what was going on."

There was also a later tour with Zodiac Mindwarp and The Love Reaction, which won the band a strong fan base, as Malc recalls: "The tour was pretty dire; Zodiac were really metal and not that funny anymore. A lot of people preferred us. The first date was at Leicester and their roady welcomed us by tapping this great big baseball bat, saying 'So YOU'RE The Wonder Stuff then...' Zod just raised his one eyebrow and never said a word to us." Miles continues "We picked up a lot of fans from bands who were getting too big to stay close to their following for various reasons, whereas we, as the support band were just doing it all at full tilt, so maybe we were a little more interesting- 'Zodiac doesn't hang out with the kids anymore but The Wonder Stuff do,' that sort of thing. Eventually of course the same thing happens to us, for example with the Ned's, and then with them and so on." Martin remembers their policy of choosing support bands: "That's when we decided to be democratic about support bands, so we all got to choose two bands each. Bob chose 'Head of David' for one, who were absolutely dreadful. We were thinking 'What the hell's this lot?' - he undoubtedly enjoyed their gig more than ours." It was on the back of such growing support that The Wonder Stuff signed to Polydor in December 1987. There was money for new gear, distribution and promotion as well as a far greater availability of studio time. However, Malcolm remembers being distinctly underwhelmed by the lack of dramatic change: "When we signed it felt exactly the same as before except that we had much better gear." Miles continues "We played a gig in Manchester with a band called 'No Man's Land,' and they turned up with seventeen flightcases, all numbered in the hallway; they were supporting us, and we were no great shakes in early '88. We were still throwing all our stuff in the back of the Transit van with a mattress...and Bob. But it was nice to be able to go to the studio when you wanted, whereas before you could only afford to go twice a year and that blew all your savings."

The debut single for the new label was 'Give Give Give Me More More More' which charted nationally at No.75. More success came with their second release, 'Wish Away' which almost made the Top Forty at No.43. Finally, in August of 1988 the band's third single 'It's Yer Money I'm After Baby' crashed into the national charts at No.40. The achievement was all the greater because they had not enjoyed any notable daytime radio play, and the video was not aired with any regularity on television. The Wonder Stuff were still too different to be acceptable to the mainstream music executives. The enormous potential which so many had now prophesied was realised when the band's debut album 'The Eight Legged Groove Machine' reached No.15 in the charts. The inspiration for this debut long- play was no more glamorous than the No.9 bus from Birmingham to Stourbridge. Writing the album itself brought some new experiences, as Martin recalls: "Recording 'The Eight Legged Groove Machine' was like going to work. Every day you'd get on the tube and go

'OOOHHHH!!!, that advert's changed since yesterday.' Also, I remember whilst we were recording, we went to see The Sugarcubes and we thought 'They're brilliant and our album's shit. Just a crap collection of songs rather than an album.' "

Studio availability was not the only eye-opener for Malc. "We couldn't believe that bands had separate rooms on tour. They all seemed to think we were like The Monkees, bunking up in one room. It was really lonely and miserable in your own room." Miles continues "..when we were demo-ing 'It's Yer Money I'm After Baby' there were four of us in one little room. All sharing the bathroom, choking because Martin and Bob would smoke until four in the morning. Everyone starting arguing because Malc spent too much time in the bathroom, and ended up moaning at Bob because he never spent any time in there at all!!" It was also at this time that the band realised that most of their label mates seemed to consist of virtually everybody they had spent the last eighteen months slagging off in public.

The band were still rehearsing in Stourbridge at this stage, despite some of them now living in London. Adam Booker, a close friend (and now the band's drum technician) was oblivious to the dangers that lay ahead for him. Martin continues "I was looking for someplace to stay and Les said there was a spare room at Ad's place." Ad offered to help and remembers how his house was soon taken over "I was invited out for this meal and half way through the night someone says 'I've got nowhere to live...' I ended up housing Martin and eventually Bob. Everyone moved in and my missus moved out. 110 Clive Road. Anybody stayed there. It was a pit." Miles continues "The front room was unusable because Ad had kicked in the window on one occassion when he had forgotten his key, so it was too cold to use. The living room had Malc's telly in it - a constant source of annoyance to Malc. I once had the unfortunate experience of sleeping three in a bed with Ad. The whole house was a wreck except for Malc's room which was immaculate - a complete safe haven, like something out of Alice in Wonderland. After gigs there'd be punters everywhere, loads of booze and fags, and Malc wouldn't let anyone near his room. I was in this lovely house in Walsall with my girlfriend, but all I wanted to do was get legless with the guys so

I'd always stay there instead. I preferred to kip on the floor with the beer cans. At this point we had very little to do with the Poppies because they were doing the world by then whilst we were still doing Redditch."

This was not strictly true. The album tour covered eighteen dates including gigs at The London Astoria, Birmingham Powerhaus, and Newcastle Riverside. Again, much experience was to be had for the band, as Miles remembers: "I hadn't discovered that when you go on tour you should get fit for it and not go on the beers everyday and smoke until four in the morning. I just felt ill all the time. But there was a great night in Aberdeen in November '88. I was asleep having a dream about a fire alarm going off, when my girlfriend wakes me up because there is a real fire in the hotel. So we all put our gear on, stuffed some Jack Daniels into our pockets to keep us warm and legged it down the stairs. I got Dave, our manager, out of bed and he's halfway down the stairs when he says 'Oh no, I've forgotten my fags!' so he runs back to get them, leaving the entire float of cash from the tour behind. All the fire engines were there by now but our group was one person short. It was a guy called Puncher who was missing, a real character - all he'd bought on tour with him was the clothes he was standing in and a Sainsbury's carrier bag full of party hats. We were really getting worried because he didn't drink so there was no way that he was too drunk to hear the alarm. Then all of a sudden he comes down the stairs in a pair of shorts and a plastic party fireman's hat going 'It's alright everybody, calm down, I've put the fire out.' They'd found him in his party fireman's hat fighting this bloody fire with a little extinguisher. They thought he was completely mad. He probably was. He didn't actually do a great deal on tour, he was mostly there for the entertainment value. He occasionally helped out with security or handed out lollipops to the kids down the front."

Unfortunately the infamous and much-documented European tour was not so much fun, and the band couldn't wait to abort. As Miles says: "It was too much - we were playing the old songs over and over again when we really wanted to be demo-ing new stuff, preferably at home. We were never into it. Unfortunately though, Ad had hitched for three days solid to meet us in

Germany, through snow , wind and rain. He finally gets there and we said 'Sorry Ad, but we're going home tomorrow.' He was not pleased." This was followed by an American tour where the band found that they had to work hard to win over audiences again. Nevertheless the efforts appeared to be worthwhile: "On our first New York gig, there was hardly any promotion and no bar - so that wiped out the floating voters and we still managed to pull 600 punters. I'd call that a success."[3] "We became famous for holidays rather than gigs - we always did about ten dates and then spent the rest of the time in a jacuzzi." Malc remembers the tour for the unusual bus driver: "He was a wanted man in three states and didn't have a licence. He used to drive for eighteen hours in a row, no problem, because all he did was snort sulphates and listen to Kiss on the radio.'

Despite the success at home and abroad, the band did not enjoy all of the tours in the winter of 1988, even though they were popular enough to sell out The Town and Country Club for two nights. This period was worsened by the fact that they were beginning to bore with playing the old material and at the same time were ever so slightly wary of the marketing machine of Polydor starting to rumble. At the end of the second T&C sell-out Miles stormed off stage and left the band to fall apart in his absence. The Bass Thing was furious and went after Miles, sacking managers and agents on his way. At the hotel the arguments continued as did the ill-feeling . This was hardly the ideal atmosphere for a band dubbed to be "on a quest to become the biggest band in the world."[4] Nevertheless they were not about to lose control, as Miles recalled: "I remember the times when me and Clint had to throw all the money onto the table to see if we had enough money to buy milk, otherwise it was black tea."[5] In one sense, the bad gigs were useful in that they left the band anticipating and looking forward to the next tour, with new material and bigger audiences.

The band came back from America to a £500 a week record company flat in London, for the purpose of recording the second album, 'Hup!' Miles and Bob nearly missed the first studio session altogether, because they'd met a group of people in New York and stayed out there: "Everyone was worried that we'd stay there period. We eventually got on the plane on the day of the recording for 'HUP!', and got back around 6.30 in the morning at Mart's house. We were supposed to be in the London flat for a month but we ended up there for nearly a year. The Poppies were working in London at the time so they stayed there as well. Fiddly Bell was in the process of joining. It was brilliant. Clubbing every night, loads of people round all the time, having a great time. Three phonelines, with certain American girlfriends phoning home all the time so the bills were massive. You could go to Paramount City or any nightclub and bring the entire club and more back for a party. We were supposed to be doing 'Hup!' It fizzled out in the end and became quite a depressing place to live. It got too much really." Even now Bob was still a law unto himself : "Bob's room was at the end of this really long corridor - 'Bob Jones and the Temple of Doom.' He'd stay in there with his video for days on end. Then this smell started to emanate from his room and we were saying 'Bob, wash some bloody clothes will you?' It turned out that there was a sewer under his bed which had leaked all under the carpet. So we all ended up in the front room me, Clint and Ad Poppie and Bob - we bought these quilts from Marks and Spencers which were thirteen Tog, so we'd just get under there and watch videos and drink beer."

.......And record an album. 'HUP!' was released in October 1989, and was followed by a national tour which Miles details as "shitty really, because Bob hated it and was always in a bad mood." The introduction of the fiddle has passed easier than Miles suspected "I always found the fiddle quite offensive. I remember seeing the Waterboys at the beginning of the year and everything was drowned out by the fiddle. I thought it was awful...I hope we haven't over-used it."[6] For Fiddly Bell the tour was more enjoyable: "I quite enjoyed it because the venues we played were a great size, like Hull City Hall. That was the last time we did a full tour of England and I think it was great for that fact. Also I ran into Billy Joe Spears after a really crap gig in Liverpool!"

The band then went to Wales to demo some new ideas for the third album 'Never Loved Elvis'. Malc recalls how they kept the locals awake at three in the morning: "We hired these bikes, got

tanked up and went to the top of this bloody great big hill in the dark with no lights. Then we'd bomb down until you couldn't pedal any faster - about 50mph. The trick was not to miss the bend at the bottom, or else you'd be in the water. On this bend, there was a white line, so the rule was 'when you see the white line turn left for God's sake.'" On a more serious note, however , things were not improving with The Bass Thing, and in December of 1989, whilst they were in Wales, he announced he was to leave The Wonder Stuff. He never really recovered from the disastrous European excursion of October 1988, and the band frequently became a second priority: "There was a time in America when we were due to play and Bob went AWOL. We had to catch our plane and leave one of our managers behind to search for him."[7] To be fair The Bass Thing himself never made a secret of his dissatisfaction. Shortly after the release of the second album he was quoted as saying "At this moment in my life I'd rather not be in a band, I'm sick of it. There's always arguments of some description, although nothing really that drastic. It would be nice just to walk away and have some time without anybody ringing up about photo sessions, interviews, recording, T.V, it hasn't stopped since 'HUP' came out."[8] This major development ironically came at a time when the band were celebrating a three night sell-out of the 3,000 seater Aston Villa Leisure Centre in their home town. Miles remembers those dates with mixed feelings: "They were very odd gigs in a way. There we were giving each other Christmas presents in soundcheck, these were our best ever dates and all the time in the back of our minds we were thinking this is probably the end of it all. Bob left straight after the third night and that was that. We all stayed at our parents for Christmas, and then I met up with Malc back down at the London flat. We both said that it didn't seem worth carrying on. Even though we had some new material, we'd never lost a member before and that was very strange. Fortunately, we decided to carry on."

By contrast though, 1989 had also provided the band's biggest successes to date - 'Hup' had charted at No.5, and went on to sell over 140,000 copies, earn a Top of the Pops debut, plus two UK tours (the second one a sell-out) with two hits in the charts. The

music press were almost falling over themselves to review the
album. Andrew Collins perhaps best summmed up The Wonder
Stuff's revival from their difficulties when he said: "..if The
Wonder Stuff were a deeply flawed, confused, legless mess following the aborted Euro-tour of '88, then 'Hup' was proof that
this was still a band to be reckoned with. If an album that clever,
that intricate and adult could come from a band so fraught with
inner conflict, personality problems, and severe maladjustment
within the Big World of Pop, then that's surely proof of character."[9] More success was waiting for the band in America, largely
due to their now blistering live set. Despite the reservations some
people had expressed about whether the peculiar music, attitude
and humour that is The Wonder Stuff would translate across the
Atlantic, the band stormed into the College Top 10 and received
excellent press from all of the twelve dates. Generally it seems
that the band enjoyed playing the American gigs, particularly as
they still find it amusing that "This all started in Cradley Heath in
the West Midlands one afternoon because we had nothing better
to do. Here we are in L.A. in a jacuzzi."[10] American audiences
received the band very enthusiastically; one reviewer described
their reaction thus: "Powering through sixty minute sets that have
their American audiences shaking like a shitting dog The Wonder
Stuff are mixing fifteen new songs with the most impressive highlights of their two years young back catalogue."[11] Despite their
success some record companies and radio stations were reluctant
to entertain the band, fearing 'punk's second coming' with room
trashing and the like. One station warned people to 'lock up your
daughters, here comes The Wonder Stuff' while another DJ took
one look at them and refused to broadcast the interview live. The
band's response to some American music was equally cautious, as
Martin commented "The Grateful Dead? You can see bands like
this in Dudley on any Sunday afternoon" "When we were in New
York we went round Central Park and I remember thinking ,
'Christ, this is a long way from Stourbridge.'"[12]

Back at home the band entered the difficult period of writing
material for the new album, whilst incorporating new members.
Early post-Bass Thing days were difficult and they were loathed
to audition hundreds of different hopefuls. Miles' brother Russ

came up with the answer and recommended ex-Libertines bassist Paul Clifford. Paul continues: "I was at University in Liverpool, and Miles' brother Russ phoned me up and said 'How do you fancy coming down to rehearse with The Wonder Stuff?' So I did and they turned round and asked me if I wanted to go to Europe on tour supporting The Mission." Miles explains "Everything had been on hold for a while after Bob left, and then here was Wayne Hussey saying 'Come on holiday with us, we'll have a great laugh,' meaning 'Do you want to come on tour with us?' As a warm-up for Paul and for ourselves we arranged some dates at Junction 10 in Walsall - we thought they would be a nice, quiet little warm up for Paul but they were basically in front of every single friend he's ever had, a real baptism of fire!" Nevertheless, despite a few problems with when the drum machine being used for 'Inertia' "went absolutely haywire with the heat" these gigs were extremely well received and clearly eased one fan's uncertainties about the transition when he was overheard as saying 'The Bass Thing's had a pretty short haircut...' Paul continues "We went to Europe and that was ideal for me to settle in because, apart from the fact that The Mission were great to tour with, absolutely nobody liked us over there and since we were supporting there was no real pressure.

The dates with The Mission then continued in America and Canada, where the roles of musical Agony Aunt were somewhat reversed, as Miles remembers: "The unfortunate thing was that there was Wayne and his lot picking us up to get into gigging again, and then we get to Toronto and while we're waiting in the airport The Mission's Tour Manager walks in and announces that the guitarist has just left and gone home. They had a spare guitarist who had been helping them out for a few numbers, so they got away with it - Malc was dragged on for a couple of numbers at one stage - suddenly there we were, doing exactly the same thing as they had done to us, trying to pick THEM up. It was on that tour that I listened to the chart countdowns on Radio One over the phone and then wondered why I had enormous hotel phone bills every time."

Towards the end of the tour the sound engineers of the two bands started to "have a few words" culminating in Malcolm walking on stage in Dallas "and there was Si, our sound man, sitting on top of this bloody great big tower in a huge cowboy hat, annoying the hell out of their soundman." More serious problems with illness caused the band to cancel the last few dates on the east coast. Miles continues: "That annoyed quite a few people so we went back to the east coast to do the gigs that we had missed, with a band called 'Too Much Joy'. They went to Florida and played the Two Live Crew set (which was banned at the time) just to get arrested and get some press - they wanted to be kick-ass bad boys but they wern't really, more like The Housemartins but without the songs or the characters. So we kicked them off the tour; then we met this band in a McDonalds in Boston, who gave us a tape. I listened to it at soundcheck and thought it was alright so backstage after the gig we were all drunk and said 'Why don't you come on tour with us?' We didn't realise how much trouble this caused for loads of agents and other people but they were well into it. They were called 'Public Works' and they had this mate with a Spacecruiser, so they followed us all the way down the east coast and right across to L.A. The last gig was in San Francisco after which we shot off to the airport and flew home. These poor blokes had to drive for three days and three thousands miles to get anywhere near home - we got back days before they did."

Although 1990 was a quiet year for releases (only one, 'Circlesquare' in May), as Miles explains this was a very deceptive view : "Publicly it was quiet but we were really into it, and were gigging like mad. We'd been talking about doing a video so we had a Super 8 camera with us on a lot of the dates, (the home videos appear on the hugely successful release 'Welcome To The Cheap Seats'), and we had all these ideas for the new material which we were really keen to start demo-ing." Fiddly continues: "We came back from America to get started on 'Never Loved Elvis' We went to The Town House Studio in Camden to demo new ideas for the album, and there was that terrible night when we lost to Germany in the World Cup. We had all the monitors switched on to the football and everything stopped. Recording was completely arranged around who was playing that particular night." Despite the lone release the band graduated to bigger

venues such as The Aston Villa Leisure Centre, Preston Guildhall, Glasgow Barrowlands and Brixton Academy. The press response was as enthusiastic as ever: "(The Wonder Stuff)..play decent, simple pop tunes, which like themselves have a rough exterior but deep down possess a heart of gold...it's time to stop underestimating The Wonder Stuff. They're pop stars with compassion, alternative role models who could, if they wanted, branch out in a big way ." Another reviewer saw them thus: "The Wonder Stuff are now looking very much like a band for whom anything is possible."[13]

Towards the end of 1990 the band had a few problems on the domestic front - the planned 'Day Of Conscience' gig along with The Mission never materialised and they fell out with The Mean Fiddler over the much-maligned New Year's Eve date with The Wonder Stuff as headliners. This all served to create quite a degree of bad feeling, as Miles explains: "By now we were really keen to sort out some big gigs. Glastonbury didn't happen and Reading was out because The Mean Fiddler promoted it, so we decided to arrange our own festival. The Bescot Park gig in Walsall was the result and it was fantastic; the reasons we were given for bands not wanting to appear on the bill were hilarious. Julian Cope said he couldn't do it because he 'couldn't get the vibes right in the daylight' and Big Audio Dynamite said it was too much of a rock bill (even though Spirit of the West, the Canadian folk band were on the bill), and that they wanted to play dance bills."

Clearly playing in front of 20,000 fans in your home town was not enough to satisfy Malcolm on its own; "The amazing thing was that we met Dave Hill out of Slade and he was asking US how we get our guitar effects - that was incredible!" At that Bescot gig there was also an appearance by Vic Reeves and Bob Mortimer whom Miles had met in the April of 1991. "I was at a play and I saw Vic so I said 'Hello.' He eventually came over and said 'We saw you play in Liverpool last year.' So I said 'We never played Liverpool last year..' and he says 'You did, I was there...you are Pop Will Eat Itself aren't you?"

"Vic quite liked the idea of being a pop star so he asked us if we were interested in doing something - he wanted to do a follow up to 'Born Free' but something a bit rockier, and came up with 'Ring Of Fire' by Johnny Cash, but the Tom Jones version. We were a little reluctant and somebody eventually came up with 'Dizzy' which I'd never even heard of, nor Malc. I wanted to do a Hawkwind cover but that would have vanished without a trace! Every time we do stuff on stage with them two it's chaos - I always end up just laughing uncontrollably. The radio mikes never work, so they lose their place and just start making up the words, and then everyone's losing it. It's mad."

The album dates were hit by 'the rain curse' which opened the heavens every time they played an outdoors gig. The British leg was brief, and was followed by more dates in America, supported by The Milltown Brothers, whose keyboard player, Barney, introduced himself by throwing up all over their dressing room beers. Not for the first time did members of the crew flaunt the United States legal system, as Miles remembers: "We did a gig where Russ and Jez got arrested for bumping a car out of the way of the exit from the venue. We came out and there's loads of police around - Adam Booker was saying 'Don't go left, whatever you do, keep away from the left', so of course we come straight out and go left to see what was going on. Anyway, they were taken away and put in the cells for a night. Being considerate types we left them there in Philadelphia, and Les our manager took care of them." Fiddly continues "They were made to watch a video telling them how to be good American citizens, and how bumping cars is such a dangerous thing to do, so we set it up that they also had to write a 5,000 word essay on what they learnt and how they were going to be reformed characters from now on - they swallowed the lot."

Despite having played in front of 20,000 in Walsall and many thousands elsewhere, this tour was not devoid of it's 'smaller' venues. "It was on these dates that we were supposed to play a big all-girls school in Boston. When we got there it was a cafe. It was some tiny student bar with room for fifty people in it, and more Dunkin' Donut machines than punters. We walked straight in and straight out again."

The British and American gigs were followed by a series of dates in Australia and then Japan towards the end of 1991. In the

case of Australia their reputation went before them, as Miles recalls: "When we arrived in Australia the Poppies had been three times before us and done a great promotion job on us - they were great gigs as a result. Japan was a different experience altogether though, and one I generally didn't like." Fiddly continues: "For the first couple of nights nobody moved or laughed or anything, it was really strange. The we discovered our 'No.1 Fan' as we dubbed him, down the front every night shouting at us in Japanese. When the rest of the crowd saw him having a good time they realised it was alright to do the same - after that it was okay but it can be so formal over there." Miles thinks this is because "they're just nervous of five big hairy gits like us. Once the ice was broken it was a lot better." 'No.1 Fan' turned up at one gig in a polka dot suit he'd had made to match Paul's, and was overwhelmed when Malc gave him his pass for all his efforts. He even tried to keep up with the tour convoy: "We had these minibuses and he would chase after us for about four miles down the road. Every night he'd wave at me before the gig and I thought he was saying 'good drugs, good drugs' so I'm saying 'I don't want your drugs, piss off.' Anyway three nights later I realised he was actually saying 'Good luck, good luck.' He was amazing. The whole thing was a total culture shock really. Did you know Mount Fuji's covered in council houses? It's unbelievable."

The overseas dates were finished at the start of December, after which the band returned home to some gigs in the UK, looking forward to the Christmas break. As Miles recalls however, their plans for an early finish were doomed: "All this time we were doing these Christmas gigs in Britain there was this Christmas gig coming up for a radio station called KRockFM in America. Ian McCulloch and The Banshees were also on the bill and the idea was that it was a totally acoustic set, despite being in front of 7,000 people. All you could have was a bass - everything else had to be acoustic. We really didn't want to do it, so we decided that I would do it on my own. I'd done some stuff with the Ned's like that in America so I wasn't too worried about it. Anyway, we did these dates in Britain, finishing with the Town and Country on the 21st December and the rest of the band all got absolutely legless because they thought it was the last date of the year. Anyway, about three o'clock, our American manager comes in and says 'They've found out Miles is doing the gig on his own and they won't have it. You've all got to go to the airport tomorrow morning at 6 o'clock and do the gig.' We managed to drag ourselves out of bed with stinking hang-overs and get down to the airport, where we were delayed for hours. When we finally got there we only had a couple of hours to spare, so we sat in this small hotel room trying to work out an acoustic set of some description. At the gig itself it turned out people were using loads of electronic gear, and all we had was two acoustics. Halfway through the gig, Billy Idol came in with his walking stick and all his entourage, women everywhere, with a spot light on him - the whole place just stood up for him. It was so funny. Anyway we got most of the press 'cos we were drunk and it went down really well."

It was at this gig that the band first met Siouxie and The Banshees and ended up touring with them in the January of 1992. Although they now see it as one of the best tours they've ever done, the start was fairly nerve-wracking: "On the second gig the Banshees manager came in and said 'Siouxie's got a really bad throat, we've got to pull the gig.' So we had to decide whether to go on in front of thousands of disgruntled Banshees fans who would probably hate us, or pull the gig - champions that we are we did the gig and it was a corker!" Miles continues: " Even though we only did forty minutes, which can be pretty difficult if you're trying to play three albums worth, it was a great tour, possibly my favourite ever. The attitude of everyone on tour was spot on. At first they stayed away from us, because of what they'd heard about our tour antics, and we thought 'They're Siouxie and the Banshees, we can't possibly talk to them.' Then on one journey Fiddly and Martin were so drunk they got on the Banshees tour bus by mistake, introduced themselves and that was that. Parties from then on, piling into dressing rooms and stuff like that. They were really nice to us."

In the spring of 1992 the fourth single from the album 'Welcome to the Cheap Seats' reached No.8 and earned a Top of the Pops appearance. The previous appearance for 'Dizzy' had been memorable, as Miles explains: "We were in America with

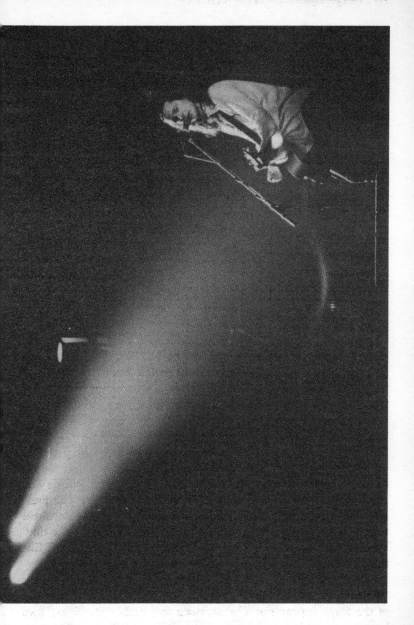

The Milltown Brothers when Island Records (who had done 'Dizzy') insisted that we do Top of the Pops. So we had to fly back straight after a really sweaty gig, via Memphis, which when you're album's called 'Never Loved Elvis' is not a good idea. For that Top of the Pops appearance we'd only just got our body chemistry sorted out. The next time we did the show for 'Cheap Seats', I went to Camden Palace the night before and the bouncer decided to punch me for some reason. Les wanted to pile in so we were holding him back, it was a right mess. So consequently I turned up for the show with a big fat lip and my jaw swollen and out of joint. Kirsty MaColl went and got some champagne and we got absolutely legless - I had to wear all this daft make-up to cover up my battle scars."

The summer of 1992 was spent doing Festivals and warm-up dates. Paul particularly enjoyed the Feile in Ireland: "The Feile was a really good day - there are no noise restrictions like Reading and the bill was a really good one, plus the Poppies were there - they seem to put more effort into it." Miles continues: "We also did a benefit gig for The Milltown Brother's guitar technician Spike, who was unfortunately killed in a road accident on tour. We played alongside The Milltown Brothers, and Crazyhead. Malc was pretty ill at the time so we had to get Loz out of Kingmaker to fill in - we gave him a week to learn all the songs and he did great. It was really weird for us though to be alongside him on stage instead of Malc. Also the rest of Kingmaker were down the front hurling abuse at him. Brilliant."

Reading '92 is viewed with mixed feelings: as Malcolm says "we got away with it, but that's not what you go to do. Going on so late with no soundcheck, the pressure of headlining, and having to entertain the crowd for an hour and a half, it's very difficult. At some stages you could tell the crowd were losing the sound." Miles nevertheless enjoyed the gig while he was onstage: "It was a thrill to do - I thought the audience were absolutely fantastic. I was happy with the gig, but maybe that was because I was drunk." Entering the winter of 1992, the band have just moved into the Far Out Recording Company's own studio which "is great because we can demo stuff straight away and keep trying things - it's just a much better environment to work in really, a lot easier." As for the new material, the band are very enthusiastic, as Miles explains: "Nobody's really expected much from The Wonder Stuff, unlike the big bands that are hyped up so much by the press. It's not the fault of these bands that they are talked about all the time and that this ruins listening to them or watching them. It's the fault of the narrow-minded, unimaginative media and it sucks. We do what we do - some of our business people talk about us being massive - the fact is that we'll do what we've always done, write a collection of songs and record them - the whole point of the band has always been primarily to entertain ourselves. If it becomes successful from that then great – I've never really seen us as part of the whole rock picture in any way and I like it that way. If we can continue in this fashion at the level we've achieved now that would be ideal. It would be nice in nine years if our tenth album was a multi-million seller but in the meantime this is just our little thing going on here, and hopefully people will find it entertaining."

STOURBRIDGE: WHAT SCENE?

"You don't want to think 'Oh, I need a pint of milk, I'd better put my sunglasses and stage gear on.'"

CLINT

CHAPTER FOUR

"Stourbridge is more of a myth than any other, and that's great in a way. If they wanted to do the press on Stourbridge they'd get here and have nothing to photo - it would be 'where's the venue, where's the scene?'" says Jonn of Ned's Atomic Dustbin. In Manchester and Liverpool for example, the press seized upon a fresh scene and investigated every aspect of it, to the extent, says Jonn of "'what's the colour of your underwear' syndrome; the Manchester scene was something that the press constructed, and they did it very well - if that's what a scene is, then Stourbridge certainly hasn't got one." The absence of a particular venue or fashion was apparent from the early days - Dave Morris of The Work Shop Studio says that "In 1987 when The Wonder Stuff first came here there was no such talk of any scene, nothing like that; it was not until later that people began to notice the great bands coming out of the area." He goes on to say "the main reason that this thing about Stourbridge exists is pride on the Poppies part, because they said 'we come from Stourbridge' and the press said 'where?', and they said 'Stourbridge, it's a great place and we're proud of it.'" Craig Jennings of Chapter 22 Records agrees: "There's no club with a ridiculously hip juke box - three bands coming from one pub is pretty amazing, but that's all there is to it really."

Part of the reason for the lack of any 'scene' is that the bands are not known to frequent much of the popular music press, particularly that which is targeted at the younger age groups. For example, Ned's declined to perform on the 'Motormouth' or 'Going Live' T.V shows or appear in 'Smash Hits'. Miles was once asked by 'Blue Jeans' magazine whether he wore boxer shorts or not - his answer is both predictable and unprintable. This section of the public have very short memories, and even shorter concentration spells, threatening bands with very brief

shelf lives - to quote Jonn: "As we get more popular our following
will get younger, and you are on dangerous ground when most of
your following are twelve year olds - that is what Jesus Jones did
wrong in Britain. They fortunately consolidated themselves
because they are so big abroad, especially Japan. Don't get me
wrong, if twelve year olds want to buy our records then great, I'm
not prejudiced, but the day I go on stage and see 2000 twelve
year olds, I'll think 'in twelve months time there will be twenty'."
This plank of intense media hype which actually destroys many
credible bands, is avoided by the Stourbridge crew - one look at
bands who have suffered from this, like Curiosity Killed the Cat,
Bros, or any number of 'tenny-bop' bands, is sufficient justifica-
tion for this much-maligned attitude.

At the same time however the music press are always eager to
use 'Stourbridge' almost as a convenience label. This is helped by
the fact that the bands find themselves easy targets for the music
press gossip columns. They are more than aware of the pros and
cons of this situation. In 1988 Rich said - "We released our first
record two years ago. We've been a high profile band and unfortunately you can say and do a lot of stupid things in two years."[1]
Clint has had other difficulties - his mother was alarmed to read
in one of the gossip columns the completely fictitious story that
he was supposed to have poked his backside out of a car window
and shit on the road. But in many ways such stories have created
a larger than life persona for the band, and have probably
increased their public exposure. Column inches such as these all
add to the hype around a band; "They are living, laughing proof
that they actually believe their favourite joke - 'What's the definition of the perfect woman? Someone who shags all night then
turns into a six pack and curry at dawn.'"[2] At the end of the day
though, the final laugh is on those who believe everything they
read.

All three bands have found that the BBC, Radio 1 and Top of
the Pops are less eager to feature them. Ned's found at their
debut performance that there was a great deal of ill-feeling
towards them, largely because of the way they looked and the
music they played. "Apart from the make-up girls (who were
great), we got a predictably cold response" says Jonn. He also

said of the experience: "All I could really think of to say was this is our song and its sold shitloads, just be proud of it. We deserve to be here." Alex felt an outsider, "like the difference between Baroque and Kraftwerk. We didn't really fit in."[3] PWEI are more enthusiastic about the show: "You have to go and show people there is a choice. If you sit at home and all you ever see is Kylie and Jason then you'll be into them (Jason more than Kylie 'cos she's shit). Whereas if you see the Wedding Present at least you have a choice." Rich puts the programe on a higher level than this - "I have a theory that no band ever lives up to it's potential until they've been on Top of the Pops, and that particular childhood dream has been purged from the system..." Graham agrees: "If you haven't been on Top of the Pops there's still that embarrassment about what you do when you go 'round your Aunty's house. 'So when are you going to be on Top of the Pops?' she'll ask. It's a real taxi driver line - if you say 'no' it's assumed that you're just a dosser and that really you are on the dole. But if you say 'yes', well...they probably think they're going to get a big tip actually. And they're wrong."[4]

The Wonder Stuff are a major band and have sold thousands of copies of three albums and nine hit singles. Yet their first major daytime airplay was for 'Size of a Cow' from their third album. 'Hup', which went on to No.5, achieved very little in terms of regular daytime airing; similarly, only now are PWEI enjoying reasonable airplay. Jonn says "people just can't get their head 'round us because we're not part of the fashion, we're not mainstream in their eyes. And yet you wouldn't believe the outrageous difference it makes to get your single daytime play the week before a release. You get a tune and people buy it because they hear it on Radio One; even DJ's will go and buy it then because they know what people are listening to and then you're in the clubs. I haven't got a problem with being on Radio 1 - mainstream music changes constantly as the different bands become popular - if we got airplay in the day it would just mean that that was the way mainstream music was progressing. It would change to us, and not the other way 'round."

If there is any single factor which ties these bands together, it is their ability and enthusiasm for playing live. PWEI have done hundreds of gigs; Ned's have followers who themselves have been to one hundred and eighty gigs - perhaps in no other group of bands has there been such prolific gigging. Tank sees this as essential to establish unknown bands: "I've taken a lot of lessons out of Mega City Four's book, especially the fact that a lot of touring early on is very important. People say 'I've heard of that band, but there's a big chance they'll have forgotten about you by Friday, unless you are playing on Friday. We did shit gigs but at least we were playing to people." Such numerous live dates have their disadvantages but ultimately Ned's see it as essential. Rat says " When you start touring you're alive and fresh, but three days in you've had it. Wherever you are, whenever, you can always go to sleep straight away on tour. One of the worst things about touring is Jonn's Tour Arse." Alex has no time for poor performances - "All they want is to see you doing your job, which is to entertain. They don't care that you're knackered and they shouldn't have to care because they they've paid £7."⁵

Jonn has no doubts that this is what makes the bands from Stourbridge so unique and so successful: "In Manchester because the press constructed that scene so well, if a new band popped up the press convinced people that they were great and people would listen, because it was hip to be into that band that week. But with Stourbridge you can't do that - where the strength lies and where the attraction is for our type of audience is live. You have got to be able to play well live, you've got to have songs to play to people. You can't just go on and look pretty." There is an underlying work ethic in the Black Country which perhaps manifests itself in these bands in this continual barrage of live dates - these bands have almost forced themselves to be successful by the sheer frequency and energy of their early live performances. Jonn himself suggests the reason the Neds have increased so enormously in popularity is that "we consistently did really good live shows. A year ago there were still a lot of doubters, but we worked very hard, got lucky with a few support slots, but basically lived up to or bettered the headline bands we were involved with." Mat has no qualms about the regularity of their live shows because he loves them: "Live I'm in my element - you fire up and touch a string and it's fucking loud. When there's 2500 people in the audience you have to stuff it down their throats, whether they want to listen or not. I'm liberated rather than embarrassed. I let a lot of very private things out and I like it when the crowd can do the same. I'd like to think it motivates someone to get off their butt and do something - they should look at me and think 'he's a berk and he can do it'."

The driving force behind The Wonder Stuff is also their ability to play and enjoy great live shows. Miles is keen to avoid becoming a stadium band, which he feels would be the antithesis of everything that The Wonder Stuff stand for - places like the NEC and Wembley Arena are in his opinion "terrible". This was the main reason behind their three festival gigs in June 1991. "There's something about little hard chairs that doesn't suit what we're doing...it's too clinical."[6] Live music is what it is all about for the band, and the frequent dearth of real live bands, both saddens and annoys them. "The live thing is where we all got our love for it like. The first band I went to see was Slade and it was amazing, and it just carried on with the punk thing which was brilliant. It was ace going to see bands that were exciting. A lot of bands got involved with a big show, all the dry ice, and who gives a fuck ? As long as the four blokes on stage are having a good time and the punters are too, you don't need it."[7] Touring is equally enjoyable: "It's brilliant, I'd much rather sit in a van and go up and down the motorway, seven of us all shouting, getting on each others nerves, listening to seven different personal hi-fi's going dumm doosh dumm doosh...(but by the end...) I can't wait to get home on a Saturday night and sit in front of the telly. But then I'll be thinking, I wish it was tomorrow and we'll be in Sheffield doing a gig."[8]

Watching people like John Lydon clearly affected The Wonder Stuff's attitude to playing live. 'Whenever I spend money to go to a gig I want to be belittled by the band, because so many people these days can play well and write good songs you need something more to stand out."[9] Martin agrees: "There's nothing more revolting than going to see a band who thanks the audience at every opportunity."....Miles once said "In Cardiff and Newcastle we had total abuse so I gave it all back - if you're not going down well at least make your songs longer and make them hate you." [10]

Great live reviews remain the staple diet of all three of these bands: "In the eyes of the most discerning ears (eh?) in the business, ie. mine, The Wonder Stuff have now displaced R.E.M as the greatest living pop group in the world, and I would gladly sell my flesh for them any day of the week…Quite legendary." "(This) jaunty little combo inspire the most rabid, fanatical following, the kind of people who wouldn't bat an eyelid at sleeping rough for the whole tour just to see their idols."[11]

Despite the enormous demands of their almost continual gigging, the Ned's still have a core following of thirty or so fans who make it to every gig. Although obviously the band "take our 'ats off to 'em", this has been known to cause problems. Occasionally, as experienced also by The Wonder Stuff, some of them can take advantage of the bands appreciation of their support to abuse the favours returned. Generally this is not a situation which Ned's have a real problem with; as Tank says "With a lot of the following it becomes a pride thing to keep coming - I think they and the band have a mutual respect for each other. At an early stage it is so important to have a few fans there; quite often it'll be just enough to break the ice with the audience if there's a few going apeshit down the front." Jonn carries on "It is a social event and it's something they love doing - all this bollocks in The Sun about Crusties worshipping us is rubbish. These people have got brains, they are not stupid. They are a bit mad for wanting to hitchhike 'round Europe, but they are not stupid. As long as they don't come in the dressing room when I've got no clothes on. They'll probably continue to come Ned's gigs, regardless of our success". The 'Crusty' does not exist despite The Sun's claims that they are "easily identifiable with baggy knee-length shorts, Doc Marten boots tied with string and greasy woven hair…They buy their clothes from Army surplus stores."[12]

It is clear there is no 'image' just as there is no 'scene'. In some cases however, there are certain ways of dressing noticeable at Ned's gigs for example - not in a fashion, image sense, rather more a mutually popular way of dressing. Jonn is uneasy about this suggestion. Mat is more receptive: "an anti-image like we've acquired is an image in itself. An image is only a perception of you in the eye of the public, so if they think we look a certain way then that's that. We've never looked for this though. Personally

I'd like to wear real flares, you know one's that suck the shit out of your legs down to the knees and then scream out 'Hey!! I'm flared, right out there.' It's the same with all this rubbish about being an indie band or not being an indie band. (Ned's were accused by some 'indie fascists' of selling out by signing to a major label). That's so hypocritical when people slag bands off for charting - we never wanted to be any type of band, we're a band and that's all that counts. On a personal level I've always been concerned about my self-image, but then again there's not a person in the world who isn't, and if they tell you otherwise they're lying. Self-prestige is unavoidable - for a long time I wouldn't take my shirt off on stage. Then we did a Junction 10 gig and it was so hot that I was actually dying. So I took my top off, but I was still thinking 'they're all thinking I'm fat'. It's all very weird because you can become self-obsessed very easily. At times it's very strange." Backstage at a secret JB's gig, Rat reveals that Ned's are acutely image conscious after all - "Shall I wear this pair of smelly shorts, or this pair of really smelly shorts." Alex is equally proud of his wardrobe: "We've all got a fine selection of vile, disgusting clothes to choose from."

The Wonder Stuff also have a very loyal fan base and it is their underlying gratitude and respect for their following that explains why these bands have such loyal live support. NME felt that there was a certain type of person following the band - "The Wonder Stuff's following is both large and loyal, an odd mix of hippies, ex-goths and pop kids. There's one guy from Lancashire, The Preston Farithful they call him. Only a matter of weeks ago he jacked in his grave-digging job to follow the foursome around the globe."[13] The band are aware that as they have grown in status they are increasingly unable to keep in touch with their fans as they used to - the ten or so regulars has now become seventy or eighty at least, and quite frequently the guest list cannot accomodate them all, inciting accusations that the band do not respect them as they used to. Quite clearly, this is not the case, although Miles admits to being wary of some of the more fanatical followers: "It's flattering, but I'm very wary of them. There's something mad about people like that."[14] "Those people (day to day workers) are stuck in a job and just go totally raving mad at weekends.

Our fans are just on a constant level of insanity."[15]

So if there is no 'scene', are these people part of the whole star-making machinery? All three bands are highly dismissive of this aspect of the music business. Clint Poppie is a prime example that all the hype is not necessarily needed - "You don't want to think 'Oh, I need a pint of milk, I'd better put my sunglasses and stage gear on.' Having to live at full tilt all the time. Maybe I'm too old for all that now."[16] He goes on "Even now I can't believe we've got what the biz calls a fan base. I really don't know who we speak to."[17] He quite clearly does not present a press face for the public; after one particular night out with NME, the journalist Danny Kelly awoke to continue the interview over breakfast to find "a decaying salad of still-worn trousers, crumpled shirt and snake riot hair, he remains sprawled in his parents chintzy couch, losing the battle against the onset of a monster headache. Meanwhile his sister is busy getting her kids ready for school. As they make their way past the prostrate figure of the sometime rock deity, she whispers..'go quietly now so as not to wake your Uncle Clinton.' "[18]

Similarly, The Wonder Stuff are notoriously averse to the so-called 'star-trap', reflected to some extent by the material on the second album 'Hup', and the title of the third album itself. This attitude is borne of their dislike for image covering up a genuine lack of talent - in one newspaper interview, Miles was quoted as saying "Elvis was no more than a reasonable talent with a decent voice who, could dance a bit"[19]. The rest, he feels, was the work of the star machine, creating an image, a characerture and a totally marketable product. Miles feels that it is often the case that such activities are to the detriment of quality music, an accusation that has been touted for many years but which the band obviously still feel is highly relevant. Fiddly admits to falling into the trap in an earlier band: "It's funny, I remember the first time I got into a professional band, I was off down to Cornwall, amplifier in the back of the car thinking 'Right, I've cracked it.' Six months later I was nearly a raging alcoholic...I just can't take the whole pop star element seriously."[20] This explains why the band won't do in-store signings, don't attend record company parties or ligs, and why Martin often signs his name 'Elvis' "because at least that way it's worth something." Miles is happy with The Wonder Stuff charting, but only on the basis of their song-writing ability. In 1988 he said "If we did (chart), it would be great just because of the way we would have done it - writing fucking good songs, playing them and getting them across to the people.. He also said: "Let's just ignore all the bollocks and entertain people and write good songs."[21] Rob Jones agreed: "Imagine how pissed off they'd be if us four ugly bastards were top of the charts."[22] Miles finds it hard to believe that anybody could look up to him or PWEI, or that "they might stick pictures on the wall or cut the lyrics out of Smash Hits and stick them in the single sleeve like I've done a million times. I can't think that anyone would think of us like I used to think of Paul Weller, Joe Strummer, or Mick Jones."[23] As he has progressed in the industry, Miles has had to come to terms with the unavoidable disadvantages of being a recognised face. In the early days he would swear at autograph hunters; "one day I was completely vicious to this poor girl in Walsall..and Clint was with me and I walked away, pissed off, after it had all happened. And Clint said 'You bastard. Imagine if you'd bumped into Joe Strummer when you were fourteen. How insecure do you feel anyway when you're that age - you'd have stayed in for months!' And he said, 'Why don't you accept that people like you?'" Sometimes this attitude can backfire, however: "I was once walking up Corporation Street in Birmingham and I knew that the two girls behind me were talking about me. At first I thought, 'Oh God' and then I thought, I'll get a bit of attitude and be really nice. So this bird eventually grabbed my shoulder and went, 'Excuse me' and I went (flicks hair back and flashes a pearly smile) 'Yes?' And she goes, 'Where'd you get those boots from?'"[24] Miles still finds it humourous that all this has happened to "me and my mates who I've been shitting about out with in pubs for the last decade."[25] Malcolm finds it can be quite worrying in itself. "Nowadays, of course we're off to California and we only think about it the day before we leave. I mean, how can you get so blase about a thing like that. It's pathetic really, ridiculous."[26]

Dave Morris suggests that by approaching it in this fashion, bands from this area avoid becoming isolated and out of touch.

"When you're in a big band like these guys, you are usually the last person to realise exactly what's happened. People talk about something you are not aware of, partly because you are a part of that thing." He fains away, however, from advocating a scene in Stourbridge. "The Wonder Stuff look exactly the same in the studio as they did when they were on stage the first time I saw them - it was never a conscious decision. Any so-called image since then has probably happened more by accident than by contrivance." Jonn himself admits a somewhat contradictory attitude to the problem. "I find it frightening, really scary - now I've realised what effect my haircut can have I'm going to grow it out. I know it's a part of being well known, but I don't understand why people want to look like somebody else. Having said that, when I was younger I desperately wanted to look like Howard Jones and Simon Le Bon. Anyway now I think I fancy growing it like a trippy hippy." Morris suggests that "sometimes it is difficult to believe all that stuff because it might be difficult to come to terms with. The Ned's struck me as really down-to-earth people who basically wanted to enjoy playing their music."

PWEI have probably experienced more press hype than most, particularly concerning the now over-used concept of 'the Grebo.' Clint is disappointed at the press over-kill: "They're very much like scruffy pigs to look at. And they've got big knobbly warts and lumps all over their long hairy faces. They are very, very ugly indeed...." "We're no different to what we ever were and when that meant grebo, then yes, we were grebo. But that definition of the word has gone, even though it was us who came up with it in the first place. As media grebos we don't fit anymore." He goes on "Grebo came from one night when I went to the pictures, I stood up in the cinema and this guy from behind goes 'Sit down you greasy bastard' so it just led to us talking about grebos." "I think Grebo is a brilliant concept. It's just been totally abused by the music press."[27]

All the bands are quick to deny the existence of a 'Stourbridge scene'. It was the Poppies who were the first to push the name of their home town, from a pride typical of the Black Country, rather than a covert ploy to fabricate a new scene, especially when faced with the infuriatingly frequent accusation of 'oh, so you're

Brummies then.' PWEI were simply keen to show that they were proud of where they came from, and for the Stuffies it was probably a convenient label at the time. Rat probably most acurately, puts it all down to the press - "They like to regionalise things, out of convenience - it did help us at first. Mind you at the end of the day you have to back it up with hard work." As Tank says "Our gigs in Tokyo sold out in an hour - now that's not part of the Stourbridge circuit...yet."

David Morris believes that maybe attitudes in the area are ideally suited to the difficulties of band politics: "A particular community, a people have a way of communicating with each other. That attitude, when you are playing music, works, that attitude towards one another. It's all about give and take in a band - you can have four individuals or you can have a band. I can't help thinking that the attitude of people in the West Midlands area, the friendliness, is reflected in these bands' success. This also means you can communicate with the people who buy your records; they think you are one of them." Jonn agrees: "It's not just press and hype. There *is* something about the Black Country, and the attitude of bands from that area. I think it's brilliant that the Poppies said that early on, even if the press have tried to label it." Mat clearly has very strong feelings towards the town - "I don't know what it is about Stourbridge, it's almost as if there's a smell or a taste about it. You know when you're in a pub and all of a sudden you can almost taste a Texan Bar, you almost had it, and you then have a craving for one. Well Stourbridge is like that, it comes back to you like that. Sometimes I'll come back off a tour and just get the bus to town and wander 'round with nowhere in particular to go. I know it sounds really crap but I love Stourbridge - when my mate tells me the fishing season's started and we'll go it can all seem so much more relevant. The worrying thing is that as we tour more and more I'm losing touch with the place, and getting very unsettled. I'd really like to think that part of that attraction is the people, the accent and the down-to-earth attitudes. With our accent for example, people lay a lot of misconceptions on you about your intelligence, but when you're in Stourbridge everyone's so friendly." Jennings says "The Poppies always come back off tour and go out with their school mates from years back - it keeps your feet on the ground if nothing else." Tank agrees: "There's something about it that people seem to identify with. The bands that have come out of Stourbridge are still pretty down to earth. Okay, if someone asks for an autograph when we've just done a photo shoot in the rain then we occasionally get stroppy. I remember when I was thirteen I asked Geoff Capes for his autograph and he looked at me and said 'Not now son' - it broke my heart I tell you, I couldn't believe it. He just walked off. 'Not now son.' The disappointment was incredible. With these bands 99% of us haven't changed." Perhaps the last word should be left to Mat: "My ambition is to earn enough money to afford to buy a house in Stourbridge - if I can grow old and fart in peace in Stourbridge I'll be a very happy man."

REVIEWOGRAPHY

POP WILL EAT ITSELF

Singles

POPPIECOCK E.P:
"Ten songs for an E.P's price; ten severley hooky songs you might be tempted to sing along with if they'd just quit kicking you around the room long enough for you to catch your breath. 'Mommy, why's that man in the headphones flopping about like a rag doll in a hurricane?'...One for your long-term faves."

'AWAY FROM THE PULSE BEAT.' USA

BEAVER PATROL:
"Okay the lyrics are dumb, loud and kind of sexist but I haven't had this much fun since I did the 'bump' to Sweet's 'Little Willy' in the 7th grade. So like, breathe heavy and reminisce."

'ROCKPOOL' USA PAUL VIAGLIANO

DEF CON 1:
"Def Con 1 could be a crock of shit or a stroke of genius. It's hard to tell really."

SOUNDS

NOW FOR A FEAST:
"PWEI are willing and able to transmute the crude, minimilast essentials of power-drill rhythm guitar, scything leads, bass 'n drums and slovenly singing into a surprisingly articulate, immediately appealing kind of ruckus. The crowning critical ingredient is the writing. The Poppies' Graham Crabb is

able to tease extraordinary mileage out of simple chord pro-
gressions much the same way Pete Shelley could in his prime.
A few strategic strokes make an enormous difference: forcible
key changes in 'Oh Grebo I Think I Love You' ; the syncopat-
ed vocal phrasing on 'Titanic Clown'. Each and every cut is
blessed with chorus hooks Crispin Glover would be hard
pressed to misplace as well as sweet, crisp, cherry pie-scrump-
tious lead vocals. Like the Buzzcocks' Steve Diggle, Poppies
guitarist Adam Mole pulls it all into focus with needlepoint
riffing that stitches a peculiar identity onto each tune."

'SPIN' BROADWAY NEW YORK USA

BULLETPROOF:
  "The Poppies have, on occasion made pop music so wonderful
  the gods themselves have wept with delight."

NME

Albums

BOX FRENZY:
"Listen to the music of Box Frenzy and you'll be shocked by its strength and sophistication...PWEI have proved repeatedly that they can write short, sharp, and snappy pop songs - despite diving into sample wonderland they haven't lost their grasp of just what a good rock song is. If their beery rise as public figures has overshadowed their songwriting ability, Box Frenzy has all it needs to re-dress the balance. The scum of Stourbridge are floating to the top."

NME

THIS IS THE DAY THIS IS THE HOUR THIS IS THIS:
"'THIS' is a million happy miles from their 'pop' origins...There are a few tracks where the Poppies stick a boot so far up the proverbial donkey's anal passage that the expression 'kick ass' takes on a whole new meaning. This record sounds like it was a lot of fun to record...PWEI have produced an LP that is this close to being a masterpiece...The result is Stourbridge's answer to Sgt. Pepper. I'd call this a concept album, the concept being the creation of a comic book without the staples."

THE POP WILL EAT ITSELF CURE FOR SANITY:
"It's the music that makes it - it's a much fuller sound, a bubbling cauldron of electronic sounds and subsonic rythymns. The music is much less in your face than previously, painting

in between the lines, expanding their already well-defined moods and ideas..an astoundingly impressive LP with a few neat touches and more than a couple of goliaths. Next up the Poppies cure for indegestion."

THE LOOKS OR THE LIFESTYLE:

"This is the Poppies wolfing everything and spewing it out everywhere,..coming straight out of South Central Stourbridge. Their titles are still mad and they're still nastier than anyone really need be. A surefire hit."

NME

NED'S ATOMIC DUSTBIN:

Singles

THE INGREDIENTS E.P:

"This is a genuine razor-blade sandwich with the side salad of your choice baby. Four nervous bursts of wanderlust...NAD play as though Iggy Pop, Gregory Corso and Richard Hell were looking over their shoulders. They play as if their lives depend on it. Electric guitar naked. Not a stitch."

MELODY MAKER

KILL YOUR TELEVISION:

"He says shit on the record and they've printed the lyric on the sleeve. It won't get played when the radio people read the words. I just wish they weren't from Birmingham..."

JIM-BOB OF CARTER USM NME

HAPPY:

"A joyful romp through psychedelic indie-grunge heaven that's catchy, charismatic, funny and frantic from beginning to end. Imagine The Cure dipped in an amphetamine-filled pit then forced to sit through the back-catalogue of Sub-pop and The Ramones six times over ...frighteningly infectious."

SOUNDS

NOT SLEEPING AROUND:

"Another-jumping-up-and-down-on-your-mate's-head-sing-a-long, with madly flailing arms...a raucous rallying call for youngsters in horrible dayglo cycling shorts and comedy dread locks."

NME

Albums

GOD FODDER:

"Mat, Rat, Dan, Jonn and Alex are The Beatles for a student bar generation, a subsidised beerstain on rock's rich tapestry...'God Fodder' finds the Ned's dressed and blessed to kill - quick-witted pop craftsmen with humour and insight."

NME

THE WONDER STUFF:

Singles

UNBEARABLE:
"On the strength of 'Unbearable' I'd say The Wonderstuff were this year's great undicovered band and next year they'll be mega!"

NME

WHO WANTS TO BE THE DISCO KING?:
"Packed full of loud guitar-based rock music for which they've become famous."

SMASH HITS

WISH AWAY:
"Michael Jackson on downers."

DAVID ESSEX NME

IT'S YER MONEY I'M AFTER BABY:
"A cheeky, chirpy happy-go-lucky hybrid of Slade, The Beatles, and the Buzzcocks, all nervous energy and manic grins with irony working overtime."

MELODY MAKER

GOLDEN GREEN:
"A hoe-down stomper stinger love song complete with banjo and the line 'shut it up you silly cow'."

BRUMBEAT

CIRCLESQUARE:

"...shimmeringly delightful and woefully neglected as a dreamy summer single."

SOUNDS

SIZE OF A COW:

"A bounce along slice of sneer-pop, almost chirpy honky-tonk boogie, a cynical pleasure ride of hooks and singalongs bemoaning life in the fame lane.."

BRUM BEAT

Albums

THE EIGHT LEGGED GROOVE MACHINE:
"Immaculately crafted, unmistakeably British pop songs, all of the requisite three-minute length. Meticulously arranged harmonies glide over jangling guitars and Miles' whine never loses its wistful working-class melancholy.."

MELODY MAKER

HUP:
"They've developed the (frantic guitar) sound, ditched the disposability and forced out the barriers of their set to give it more space and depth. Instead of the Long Ball Simple Game, they've got a bit tricky, used a bit more ingenuity...'Hup' should be seen, at the end, as The Wonder Stuff coming through with colours shining like an insane kaleidoscope..I wouldn't swap my copy for three Tears for Fears albums."

NME

NEVER LOVED ELVIS:
"This is 'up' music...it soars without shame and revels in its own ability..'Never Loved Elvis' is The Wonder Stuff's best album..top hole, as Miles and no-one else in the whole world would say."

NME

DISCOGRAPHY

DISCOGRAPHY:

POP WILL EAT ITSELF:

Title	Date	Gallup/ Indie	Label
SINGLES:			
'POPPIES SAY GRRR!!!'	6/86		DESPERATE RECORDS
'POPPIECOCK'	10/86	-/5	CHAPTER 22
'SWEET SWEET PIE'	1/87	100/3	CHAPTER 22
'THE COVERS E.P.' ('LOVE MISSILE F1-11')	5/87	78/2	CHAPTER 22
'BEAVER PATROL'	9/87	76/3	CHAPTER 22
'THERE IS NO LOVE BETWEEN US ANYMORE'	1/87	66/2	CHAPTER 22
'DEF CON 1'	7/88	63/1	CHAPTER 22
'NOW FOR A FEAST'	12/88		CHAPTER 22
'CAN U DIG IT'	2/89	38	RCA
'WISE UP SUCKER'	4/89	41	RCA
'VERY METAL NOISE POLLUTION'	9/89	45	RCA
'TOUCHED BY THE HAND OF CICCIOLINA'	6/90	28	RCA
'DANCE OF THE MAD'	10/90	32	RCA
'X Y + ZEE'	1/91	15	RCA

'92° FAHRENHEIT'	5/91	23	RCA
'KARMADROME'	5/92	17	RCA
'BULLETPROOF'	8/92	24	RCA

ALBUMS:

'BOX FRENZY'	10/87	-/5	CHAPTER 22
'THIS IS THE DAY THIS IS THE HOUR THIS IS THIS'	5/89	24	RCA
'THE PWEI CURE FOR SANITY'	10/90 (RE-RELEASED 6/91)	33	RCA
'THE LOOKS OR THE LIFESTYLE'	9/92	15	RCA

NED'S ATOMIC DUSTBIN:

SINGLES:

'THE INGREDIENTS E.P'	4/90	-/-	CHAPTER 22
'KILL YOUR TELEVISION'	7/90	53/1	CHAPTER 22
'UNTIL YOU FIND OUT'	10/90	51/2	CHAPTER 22
'HAPPY'	2/91	16	FURTIVE
'TRUST'	9/91	21	FURTIVE
'NOT SLEEPING AROUND'	9/92		FURTIVE

ALBUMS:

'GOD FODDER'	4/91	4	FURTIVE
'ARE YOU NORMAL?'	10/92		FURTIVE

THE WONDER STUFF:

SINGLES:

'THE WONDERFUL DAY E.P'	2/87	-/-	THE FAR OUT RECORDING COMPANY
'UNBEARABLE'	12/87	-/9	THE FAR OUT RECORDING COMPANY
'GIVE, GIVE, GIVE ME MORE, MORE, MORE'	4/88	72	POLYDOR
'WISH AWAY'	7/88	43	POLYDOR
'IT'S YER MONEY I'M AFTER BABY'	9/88	40	POLYDOR
'WHO WANTS TO BE THE DISCO KING?'	3/89	28	POLYDOR
'DON'T LET ME DOWN GENTLY'	9/89	19	POLYDOR
'GOLDEN GREEN'	11/89	33	POLYDOR
'CIRCLESQUARE'	5/90	20	POLYDOR
'SIZE OF A COW'	4/91	5	POLYDOR
'CAUGHT IN MY SHADOW'	5/91	18	POLYDOR
'SLEEP ALONE'	8/91	43	POLYDOR
'DIZZY' With Vic Reeves	10/91	1	POLYDOR
'WELCOME TO THE	2/92	8	POLYDOR

CHEAP SEATS'

ALBUMS:

'THE EIGHT LEGGED GROOVE MACHINE'	8/88	15	POLYDOR
'HUP!'	10/89	5	POLYDOR
'NEVER LOVED ELVIS'	6/91	3	POLYDOR

FOOTNOTES

CHAPTER ONE:

1. 'APOPALYPSE NOW!' D.KELLY NME 29/04/89
2. 'HOME, HOME ON DERANGED' A.SMITH MELODY MAKER 20/10/90
3. RECORD MIRROR 11/08/87
4. COUNTY EXPRESS 09/82; MUSIQUE 01/83; BRUM BEAT 01/83
5. 'POP WILL CHOKE ITSELF' J.BROWN SOUNDS 25/04/87
6. BRUM BEAT
7. 'FOOD FOR THOUGHT' A.STRICKLAND RECORD MIRROR 06/08/88
   '2,000 LIGHT ALES FROM HOME' G.MARTIN NME 10/06/87
8. A.SMITH op.cit 20/10/90
9. 'HAIRY MONSTERS' I.BIRRELL MELODY MAKER 28/06/86
10. 'THE RIGHT TO CHEWS' T.STAUNTON NME 28/06/86
11. LIVE REVIEW T.STAUNTON NME 14/06/86
12. LIVE REVIEW G.S.KENT SOUNDS 10/01/87; I.BIRRELL op.cit
    28/06/86
13. 'REVENGE OF THE KILLER BANANAS' S.WELLS NME 03/10/87
14. 'BUMS AWAY' S.BAILIE RECORD MIRROR 16/05/87
15. 'POPPORTUNITY KNOCKS' R.WILKINSON SOUNDS 10/10/87
16. 'THE LIGHT FINGERED WAY TO FAME 'N' FORTUNE' RON ROM;
    'HOUSE OF DOLLS' A.LEWIS 11/12/87
17. LIVE REVIEW PETE PAISLEY;
18. LIVE REVIEW J.BROWN NME 23/01/88
19. LIVE REVIEW J.BARRON NME 28/11/87
20. 'RED ALERT' I.DICKSON SOUNDS 23/7/88; Ibid; 'POPPISTROIKA
    WILL EAST ITSELF' J.BROWN NME 11/06/88; Ibid; I.DICKSON
    op.cit 23/07/88
21. A.STRICKLAND op.cit 06/08/88
22. THE SPORT 17/08/88
23. D.KELLY op.cit 29/04/89
24. A.SMITH op.cit 20/10/90
25. J.BARRON op.cit 28/11/87
26. LIVE REVIEW E.TRUE MELODY MAKER 07/09/91
27. LIVE REVIEW T. SOUTHWELL NME 13/06/92
28. SINGLE REVIEW NME 29/08/92
29. 'STOMACH PUMPERS' I.GITTINS MELODY MAKER 07/02/87
30. 'CANOE DIG IT' J.BARRON NME 06/10/90

CHAPTER TWO:

1. `RUMMAGING IN THE BASS BIN' R.WILKINSON SOUNDS 16/02/91
2. NME SINGLE REVIEW 07/07/90
3. LIVE REVIEW NME CHRISTMAS EDITION 1990
4. `NED'S ATOMIC DUSTBIN' C.CLERK MELODY MAKER 14/12/91

CHAPTER THREE:

1. `STUFF `N' NONSENSE' A.STRICKLAND RECORD MIRROR 09/01/88
2. Ibid.
3. `MALICE IN WONDERLAND' J.BROWN NME 06/05/89
4. BRUM BEAT 1990
5. J.BROWN op.cit 06/05/89
6. `WONDERING MINSTRELS' T.STAUNTON NME 23—30/12/89
7. 'ELVIS ? HE'S NOT SUCH A WONDER", A. RICHARDSON, EXPRESS AND STAR 06/91.
8. T.STAUNTON op.cit 23—30/12/89
9. `WHEN THE GOING GETS TOUGH...' A.COLLINS NME 05/05/90
10. `ONE DAY MY SONS...' A.DEEROY Q 07/89
11. J.BROWN op.cit 06/05/89
12. T.STAUNTON op.cit 23—30/12/89
13 Live review, P Moody, Sounds 15/12/90; A. Mueller, Melody Maker, 18/8/90

CHAPTER FOUR:

1. `RED ALERT' I.DICKSON SOUNDS 23/07/88
2. J.BROWN op.cit 25/04/87
3. `GOD'S DUSTBIN' D.KHAN RAGE 28/03/91
4. MELODY MAKER 20/10/90
5. D.KHAN op.cit 28/03/91
6. MARK GOODIER INTERVIEW ON RADIO ONE 03/06/91
7. `IT'S A WONDERFUL LIFE' A.DARLING MELODY MAKER 20/02/88
8. A.HURT op.cit 09/07/88
9. A.STRICKLAND op.cit 09/01/88
10. J.BROWN op.cit 09/04/88
11. J.BROWN op.cit 06/05/89; LIVE REVIEW GLASGOW BARROWLANDS T.STAUNTON 28/10/89; LIVE REVIEW I.WATSON MELODY MAKER

12. THE SUN NEWSPAPER
13. S.CHAMPION op.cit 23/07/88
14. THE STUD BROTHERS op.cit 02/09/89
15. S.CHAMPION op.cit 23/07/88
16. MELODY MAKER 20/10/90
17. D.KELLY op.cit 29/04/89
18. Ibid.
19. A.RICHARDSON op.cit 06/91
20. T.STAUNTON op.cit 23—30/12/89
21. SPENCER op. cit 03/09/88
22. S.SUTHERLAND op.cit 10/09/88
23. J.BROWN op.cit 06/05/89
24. M.SCANLON op.cit 03/03/90
25. J.BROWN op.cit 06/05/89
26. `SHRINK RAP' MELODY MAKER 16/09/89
27. R.WILKINSON op.cit 10/10/87; `HEY, HEY WE'RE THE
    GREBOS' R.MORTON RECORD MIRROR 15/11/86; I.DICKSON
    op.cit 23/7/88; G.MARTIN op. cit 13/06/87